✶ THE ART OF ✶
THROWING

AMANTE P. MARIÑAS, SR.

With a foreword by JOE "BROKENFEATHER" DARRAH

THE ART OF THROWING

THE DEFINITIVE GUIDE TO THROWN WEAPONS TECHNIQUES

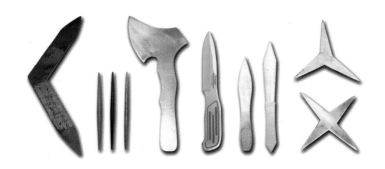

TUTTLE Publishing

Tokyo | Rutland, Vermont | Singapore

Please note that the publisher and author(s) of this instructional book are NOT RESPONSIBLE in any manner whatsoever for any injury that may result from practicing the techniques and/or following the instructions given within. Martial arts training can be dangerous—both to you and to others—if not practiced safely. If you're in doubt as to how to proceed or whether your practice is safe, consult with a trained martial arts teacher before beginning. Since the physical activities described herein may be too strenuous in nature for some readers, it is also essential that a physician be consulted prior to training.

Published by Tuttle Publishing, an imprint of Periplus Editions (HK) Ltd.

www.tuttlepublishing.com

Library of Congress Cataloging-in-Publication Data for the previous edition

Marinas, Amante P.
  The art of throwing : theory and practice / Amante P. Mariñas, Sr. -- 1st ed.
    xiv, 111, [2] p. : ill. ; 23 cm.
  Includes bibliographical references.
  ISBN 0-8048-3787-2 (pbk.)
  1. Knife throwing. 2. Martial arts weapons. I. Title.
  GV1096.M26 2006
  796.8--dc22

                              2006035534

ISBN 978-0-8048-4093-4

Distributed by

North America, Latin America & Europe
Tuttle Publishing
364 Innovation Drive
North Clarendon, VT 05759-9436 U.S.A.
Tel: 1 (802) 773-8930
Fax: 1 (802) 773-6993
info@tuttlepublishing.com
www.tuttlepublishing.com

Japan
Tuttle Publishing
Yaekari Building, 3rd Floor,
5-4-12 Osaki Shinagawa-ku, Tokyo 141-0032
Tel: (81) 3 5437-0171; Fax: (81) 3 5437-0755
sales@tuttle.co.jp
www.tuttle.co.jp

Asia Pacific
Berkeley Books Pte. Ltd.
3 Kallang Sector #04-01
Singapore 349278
Tel: (65) 67412178; Fax: (65) 67412179
inquiries@periplus.com.sg
www.tuttlepublishing.com

24 23 22   10 9 8 7 6 5

Printed in Malaysia   2111VP

TUTTLE PUBLISHING® is a registered trademark of Tuttle Publishing, a division of Periplus Editions (HK) Ltd.

"Books to Span the East and West"

Tuttle Publishing was founded in 1832 in the small New England town of Rutland, Vermont [USA]. Our core values remain as strong today as they were then—to publish best-in-class books which bring people together one page at a time. In 1948, we established a publishing office in Japan—and Tuttle is now a leader in publishing English-language books about the arts, languages and cultures of Asia. The world has become a much smaller place today and Asia's economic and cultural influence has grown. Yet the need for meaningful dialogue and information about this diverse region has never been greater. Over the past seven decades, Tuttle has published thousands of books on subjects ranging from martial arts and paper crafts to language learning and literature—and our talented authors, illustrators, designers and photographers have won many prestigious awards. We welcome you to explore the wealth of information available on Asia at **www.tuttlepublishing.com**.

DEDICATION

To my brothers and sisters Milagros, Ernesto, Patricia, Remigia,
Pilar, Teodorico, Wilhelmina, Romulo, Manolo and Marissa

In honor and in loving memory of my mother, Carolina Paclarin-Mariñas

In honor and in loving memory of my father, Virgilio Mariñas

In honor and in loving memory of my brother, Kuyang Pidiong,
who helped me with my English when I was in grade school

How to access the free online video tutorials for this book:

1. Make sure you have an Internet connection.
2. Type the URL below into your web browser:

https://www.tuttlepublishing.com/the-art-of-throwing-videos

For support, you can email us at info@tuttlepublishing.com.

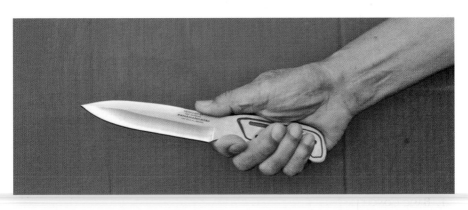

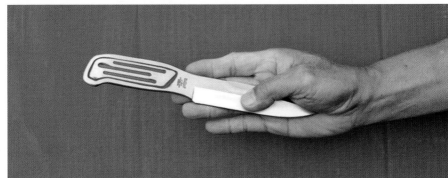

CONTENTS

ACKNOWLEDGMENTS

I gave classes during weekends when I lived in Queens, New York. In one of my training sessions, I mentioned that I intended to write a book on knife throwing. A couple of weeks later, Spencer Gee gave me two books on the subject and tasseled Chinese throwing darts.

During water breaks, my students usually asked me what my current projects were. At one time, I told my class that I wanted to make a bagakay and a throwing disk but did not have any tools. Ueli Laeng came forward and asked if I could give him the specifications. I did and gave him wood for the bagakay, and thought nothing of it afterwards. A couple of weeks later, he came to class with several bagakays and disks. I did not know that he was a supervisor in a machine shop.

On one of my birthdays, a family friend gave me a mean-looking knife—the AK-47 bayonet. I teach knife fighting and I showed my class the bayonet and then mused aloud that I would have to do a lot of walking in the process of learning how to throw it. That year, sometime in November, I received a box with ten older versions of the AK-47 bayonet. That really made my Christmas. Thanks, John.

In 1997, I decided to move to Fredericksburg, Virginia. My students gave me a going-away party at Flushing Meadows Park—and presents. I got a book on the throwing of the shuriken and a camera from Spencer; a knife throwing book and two throwing axes/darts from Tracy Pearce, and a printer to replace my broken one, courtesy of several students who pooled their resources together.

Not long after I moved to Fredericksburg, a number of students from the surrounding area came to train with me. They are no less generous than my students in Queens.

Steve Charlson gave me knives and a pair of sais. I threw them—not away—but at cardboard targets.

In 1999, I designed a knife. At that time, I only knew how to make wooden knives. Peter Sampogna and Ueli fabricated the steel knives for me. One of the knives, the VM Bulalakaw, is now marketed by United Cutlery.

One of my friends, Orlando Davidson, fabricated the first ax that I designed. Later, I designed and fabricated my throwing axes. I had only a hacksaw to cut the steel and in the process, I abused my hands. Tracy, Larry Schnitzer and Rob Mulligan sent me rotary cutting tools to save my fingers.

I have students in Fredericksburg who went out of their way to bring me the very important cardboard boxes. Two of our family friends, Lina Chan and

Francine Moore, would simply toss the cardboard over the fence and I had to make phone calls to find out whom to thank. Thoraya and Wayne Chenault brought me plywood. Wayne also loaned me his belt sander.

A virus ruined my graphics software, and for some time, I had a problem making sketches for my manuscripts. Thoraya Zedan got an updated version of the software for me for a third of its market price. She later gave me a desktop and then a laptop computer to replace my old one. Thoraya also gave me a metal detector when I was having problems finding my throwing knives in the grass in my backyard.

Anette Veldhuyzen took the photographs for the Methods of Throwing and Mechanics of the Throw sections of this book. Thoraya Zedan took all the other photographs. Anette also gave me western darts.

It took me about three years to complete the text of this work—but only because I am fortunate to have many generous friends and students. Without them, it would have taken me longer. I owe all a thousand thanks.

Books, knives, axes, wood, computers, cameras and cardboard boxes were all essential in the completion of this work. The other important element was time. For this I must thank my sisters-in-law, Olivia Tan and Sylvia Chase, for the many hours that they have saved me.

I owe special thanks to my wife Cherry and my son Amante Jr. for giving me all the time I needed to write this book.

FOREWORD

It is with mixed emotions of humbleness and pride that I find myself asked to write the foreword for a book by a person I both admire and am in awe of. I also ask myself if I am worthy or if there might not be a better person who is more qualified than I to write this?

I write this with much thought and hope that a small piece of the soul of what I am saying reaches each person who reads this book and may wonder if they are capable of making the commitment that few people are willing to endure: the time, energy, and vigor that Apo Amante P. Mariñas Sr. has put into his arts! (Apo means grandfather.)

I had the very good fortune to attend a seminar in stick and knife fighting in New York City that Po (usually the A is dropped from Apo) put on and was honored to award him his Plaque for his induction into the International Knife Throwers Hall of Fame (IKTHOF) along with one of my personal Damascus throwing knives.

Mat immediately made me feel very comfortable and welcome and was gracious enough to include me in many of his demonstrations even though most of the people there were masters in their own right of his amazing Pananandata system which he developed through his family's Filipino fighting system.

While I had very limited knowledge of the advanced techniques he was demonstrating, he was gracious enough to have his top students work with me so I at least got a rudimentary understanding and I began to feel much more at ease, having learned several other styles of martial arts over the years. But since this book is about knife throwing and knife throwers, I felt very confident in my abilities and that was bolstered by the teacher's desire to understand other concepts.

Having been a knife thrower myself for 45 years and a professional circus thrower, as well as knife maker, we came to discuss many things and I discovered that he has put an amazing amount of time and effort in his work to try to share his knowledge with the rest of the world. I learned a lot that day from a very unassuming gentleman who was very soft spoken but had the same passion as I for this incredible art/sport of knife throwing that is rapidly progressing— and for that I am extremely indebted to him!

Thank you Mat for all you have given all of us, including the future generations who will only know you through the thousands of words you have written down for them!

JOE DARRAH
Brokenfeather
Custom Knives

PREFACE

"The journey of a thousand miles starts with the first step." So the saying goes. But then, if you thought about how far *that* thousand miles is, compared to the length of one step, there is a good chance that you will never get there. One day, I sat down and estimated the distance I had covered throwing knives and other implements; I knew I had walked a lot, but I did not know how far. After some arithmetic, I calculated that I had traveled 1,600 miles.

I did not set out to walk 1,600 miles. I merely wanted to learn to throw a knife and hit the target. Indeed, my first goal was a modest one: I merely wanted to throw a knife ten times and experience how it feels.

I continued until I had thrown that knife 100 times. Even though I was missing more than hitting my target, it felt good. Then, I aimed to throw 500 times and achieved it. Modest goals, but they were significant steps. After that I became ambitious and set my sights at 1,000 throws.

I started hitting the bull's-eye, and, many times I called my son and my wife out to look at where I hit the target. Eventually, however, I had to stop calling them because I was hitting the bull's-eye very often, and it was taking too much time from my wife's and my son's work. Hitting the eye of my paper target became an ordinary occurrence.

My next goal was to throw 10,000 times—which I did. I hit the ceiling of my basement in Queens, New York quite often in getting to that milestone. Then I set another goal: 50,000 throws. I was so elated when I reached this milestone that I cut away my circular target, placed it in transparent plastic, and kept it in a binder.

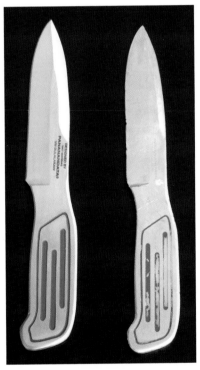

At right is the VM Bulalakaw I used for my millionth throw. I have thrown this particular knife about 100,000 times. At left is a brand new VM Bulalakaw. The initial VM is to honor the memory of my father. The VM Bulalakaw, a knife that I designed, is being marketed by United Cutlery Corporation.

I kept on throwing. I also kept a daily log of my observations, my frustrations and elation from the very first throw that I recorded. That later became the basis of my first book on knife throwing

I started writing this work when I got past 600,000 throws. When I got to 921,000 throws, the book became not merely one on knife throwing but one on *the art of throwing*.

I now throw in Fredericksburg, in a backyard that is 50' wide and 100' deep. I have more freedom to try new throws and heavier implements. I spent more than 3,500 hours throwing knives and other implements in the course of completing this work. In the process, I used cardboard targets, which when stacked, would be about 120 stories high.

I did not aim to throw knives a million times. I merely wanted to throw ten times. As it turned out, my first ten throws were my "first step" in a very long journey. I have since thrown knives and other implements more than 1,300,000 times.

I still have the circular target I preserved in that binder. I look at it from time to time with eyes that have been operated on and with brows that have deeper furrows. Did I get older?

In the village where I grew up, there is a saying, "Only the water buffalo grows old."

INTRODUCTION

I threw about 500,000 times in my basement in New York City and was able to make most any knife stick on my target. Indeed, I even threw the Philippine *balisong* (butterfly knife) hitting at an average of 96 percent. With the bagakay, I was hitting even better—over 98 percent.

I felt I had reached the limit of my accuracy with the right-hand overhand throw. The only challenge it presented me was the use of a different throwing knife. Hence, I decided to learn other throws using different grips and different throwing methods.

My first month of throwing underhand with my right hand gripping the knife by its handle was quite frustrating. However, 40,000 throws later, I was hitting with an average of 97 percent. I was satisfied with this average. I decided to learn to throw underhand with my left hand, although I had my doubts. However, 40,000 throws later, I was hitting with an average of 97 percent. I asked myself, "What next?"

I teach knife fighting. One of the knives I train with is the AK-47 bayonet. The AK-47 bayonet or any army-type knife can be held in the forward grip where the fingers are wrapped around its thick and almost flat handle. It is the grip that would be used in hand-to-hand combat. So, I decided to learn to throw the AK-47 underhand using the hand-to-hand combat grip. (I do not envision carrying an AK-47 bayonet on my person. However, throwing the AK-47 bayonet presents a challenge in two ways: it is heavy and it is not designed to be thrown.)

I couldn't wait to become good at it. So I threw the AK-47 bayonet about 400 times a day. My right arm started to hurt. For this reason, I had to let up and reduce the number of my throws. However, that did not fit with my goal of throwing knives and other implements a million times. Hence, I decided to learn other throws with my left hand. I reasoned that if I threw with my left hand, I could give my right hand a rest.

Again, I couldn't wait to master my overhand left-hand throw. My left arm started to hurt. By this time, my right arm was feeling fine. Finally, I found a balance between achieving my goal and keeping my arms pain-free. I alternated between left- and right-hand throws and between overhand and underhand throws.

I was about to fall asleep one night when a thought occurred to me: There are two ways of holding the AK-47 bayonet in hand-to-hand combat. I am already throwing it in the forward hold. I got up, took my AK-47 bayonet, and held it the other way: in the ice-pick grip.

The next day, I started throwing the AK-47 bayonet in the ice-pick grip from 20 feet. I have not stopped throwing it since.

I am now throwing the ax and the bagakay using the same throwing methods I use with my knives.

To experience something new, I decided to study a selected number of the throwing implements and methods from the Japanese and Chinese martial arts.

I had many doubts about learning new throws, throwing new implements, and learning new grips. Most of the things I worried about did not happen. I found that seemingly difficult throws can be learned by simply trying.

- CHAPTER 1 -

⟨⟩◇⟨⟩

BASIC CONCEPTS

Nobody taught me how to throw a knife. I had to learn from my mistakes. You can, too. And I can help.

You need several basic things: a good knife (or other throwing implements), a safe area to throw the knife, time, and patience. Equipped with these basic things, you can learn to throw. All it takes is practice to hit the target consistently and accurately. But, of course, to become skilled, you will need to understand and learn the basic concepts of knife throwing.

These concepts are discussed in detail. They include:

1. Grips. In seminars and classes I have conducted on knife throwing, the most common first question is, "How do I hold the knife?"
2. Methods of throwing. Right-handers will throw naturally from over the right shoulder and left-handers from over the left shoulder. From this starting point, we will cover throwing overhand and underhand.
3. Mechanics of the throw. This section covers the step-by-step actions that make up the throw.
4. Spins and rotations. For years, my teaching approach had been, "As a beginning knife thrower, it is not necessary to know how many spins happen or how the knife rotates as it streaks toward the target. This is mental clutter." However, I have since found that an explanation of the spins and rotations of the throwing implement seems to have a reassuring effect on the beginning knife thrower.
5. Throwing and sticking distances. One of my students said, "I

have the knife that you designed; I have a pretty big back-yard. But how far should I be from the target?" Good question. This section covers that critical distance.

6. Targets. Most of my students initially say that they will set up a target made of wood. Then it's my turn to ask, "How far is your nearest neighbor?" You would not want to disturb your neighbor with the sound of the impact of a badly thrown knife on wood. I will cover what materials to use and how to make the best of your space.

7. Tracking your progress and learning curves. If you become serious about learning how to throw, you will want to keep track of your progress. The *learning curve* will give you a quantitative measure for your sticks and misses.

Throwing a knife or any pointed implement is fun if you are able to make it stick and hit the target you aim at. However, you will have to be prepared to experience a sort of emotional roller coaster. There will be many ups but more downs—initially. This emotional roller coaster ride can be made visible by keeping score, that is, by counting your sticks and misses and then generating your learning curve.

Initial efforts to learn a new throw, a new method of throwing, or throwing a new implement are at the same time exasperating and exhilarating. For example: The most difficult implement to throw in my experience is the Chinese flying dart (Figure 109). It has an odd shape, and you cannot grip it the way you would a knife.

In my first 100 throws of the flying dart, I was only able to make it stick four times. Not bad. My next 100 throws were twice as successful. I was able to make the dart stick eight times. I felt good. However, my next 100 throws were not any better.

On the sixth day, I was elated. I was able to stick the dart thirty times out of a hundred. But on the twelfth day, I had a downturn. I managed to stick the dart only eighteen times out of a hundred tries.

All knife throwers will experience these ups and downs. You might decide to stop throwing when it might seem that you are not improving. Don't. Eventually with practice, you will become consistent and accurate. However, let me warn you. Practice does not make perfect. It can only get you to the limit of your ability. In the language of mathematics—to your horizontal *asymptote*.

Despite this personal limit, you will find knife throwing fun, relaxing, and challenging done alone, in competition, or in the company of friends who share the same interest.

GRIPS

The grip for any throwing implement will depend on its design. For example, there is a marked difference between your grip on a spear and on a negishi-ryu shuriken.

Most throwing implements can be gripped by the blade or by the handle. However, this only indicates which part of the implement is gripped, not how the fingers are positioned. For example: Figures 1 and 2 are both blade grips. Yet, they are very different. Hence, we have to describe the initial position of the fingers (Figures 3–6).

HANDLE AND BLADE GRIPS

These are fairly obvious when used on a knife or on an ax where the handles are distinct. However, the definitions implied by these grips cannot be applied to other throwing implements such as the spear.

We do not associate a "handle" grip with a spear although we hold it in approximately the same place each time it is thrown. Neither do we normally associate a "handle" or a "blade" grip with a two-pointed throwing dart. We do not consider a two-pointed throwing dart to have a handle.

We can however associate a handle grip with a one-pointed dart such as the Japanese negishi-ryu shuriken. But we cannot do the same with the Chinese flying dart where you will be hard put to determine where the handle ends and the blade begins.

Any attempt to associate a handle or a blade grip with the multiple-pointed shaken will fail miserably. However, the use of the terms handle (where the sticking point is toward the front) or blade (where the sticking point is toward the thrower) grip is very useful for one-pointed throwing implements.

POSITIONS OF THE FINGERS

It is not adequate to describe a grip by stating that the implement is held by the blade or by the handle. The grip must be specified by noting the initial position of the fingers on the throwing implement. In this regard, the more common grips include:

1. Curled finger grip. The four fingers are curled and the thumb squeezes the implement on the opposite side.
2. Straight finger grip. The four fingers are held straight and the thumb squeezes the implement on the opposite side.

FIGURE 1.

Blade grip

FIGURE 2.

Blade grip

FIGURE 3.

Curled finger grip

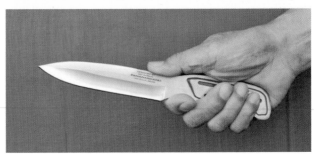

3. Wraparound grip. The fingers are wrapped around the handle of the implement with the thumb pressing on the index finger.

4. Three-finger grip. The implement is held only with the index and middle fingers and the thumb.

5. Four-finger grip. The implement is held with the first three fingers and the thumb.

These and other unique grips are illustrated and discussed in more detail in later sections.

FIGURE 4.

Straight finger grip

FIGURE 5.

Wraparound grip

FIGURE 6.

Three-finger grip

METHODS OF THROWING

A knife can be thrown overhand or underhand. The overhand throw is the method most commonly used and written about.

I am right-handed, but I throw underhand and overhand with my left and right hands.

OVERHAND THROW

I throw the knife overhand in two different ways: from above my right shoulder (Figure 7) and from above my left shoulder (Figure 8).

FIGURE 7.

The overhand throw with the knife over the right shoulder.

FIGURE 8.

The overhand throw with the knife over the left shoulder.

FIGURE 9.

The underhand throw with the knife beside the right leg.

FIGURE 10.

The underhand throw with the knife beside the left hip.

There is more freedom of movement with a throw originating from above the same shoulder as the throwing hand. The knife can be thrown with its blade hitting the target vertically, diagonally, or horizontally. I do not throw the ax on a horizontal.

Your choice of throwing method can result from the throwing area available to you. For example: If you throw indoors such as in a basement with a low ceiling, you will have little headroom. To avoid putting holes in your ceiling, you will have to throw your knife overhand on a diagonal or on a horizontal—or by using the underhand throw.

A not-so-common overhand throw is the one that originates over the opposite shoulder as the throwing hand. I use this throw from 17 feet give or take a few inches.

UNDERHAND THROW

In the overhand throw, you can use your index finger or thumb as a pointer at the time you release the knife. In the underhand throw, this is not possible. You have to rely on feel as to when to release the knife. Perhaps it is this difference in the point of reference that makes knife throwers prefer to throw overhand; the "feel" for when to release the knife is not easily acquired. Indeed, it comes only after thousands of throws. Still, with practice, your underhand throw can become as accurate as your overhand throw.

I throw the knife underhand either from beside my right leg (Figure 9) or from beside my left hip (Figure 10). From beside my right leg, I throw the knife on a diagonal, on a horizontal or on a near-vertical plane. Obviously, the underhand throw will be ideal when you throw small, light (at least 6 ounce) knives in a room with a low ceiling.

The underhand throw is not any more difficult to learn than the overhand throw. If you are already skilled in the overhand throw, you will be surprised at how quickly you will learn the underhand throw.

MECHANICS OF THE THROW

If you are a beginning knife thrower, you will first have to learn to throw the knife with enough speed to get it to the target. Then you have to learn to control the rotation of the knife so that it will get to the target point first.

To make the knife (or any throwing implement) get to the target point first every now and then is not difficult. However, for you to stick the knife consistently and accurately, you must throw it in the same consistent way in each throw. That is, the mechanics of the throw, the body and arm movements, must be nearly the same from one throw to the next.

The mechanics of a throw can be broken down into five stages: stance, the windup or the swing back, the swing forward, the release, and the follow-through.

STANCE

For a right-hand throw originating from the right side of the body, as a general rule, the left foot should be in front. For a right-hand throw originating from the left side, the right foot should be in front. This will allow for a body twist that will lend power to the throw and ensure a stable base.

The distance between the big toe of the rear foot and the heel of the front foot should be about 1½ times the length of your foot. If you do not find this comfortable, try a wider or a narrower distance.

The bend in the knee must also feel comfortable. It should be more pronounced for the underhand than in the overhand throw. This bend will allow you to raise your body weight in the underhand throw and to lower it in the overhand throw ensuring a powerful delivery of the knife.

The relative positions of your feet will depend on whether you are throwing overhand or underhand. When I throw overhand, my feet form an "L" that becomes a "V" at the completion of my throw. When I throw underhand, I set my feet in a "V" to allow my knife to clear my knee and to avoid putting a hole in my pants or cutting my leg. The "V" narrows at the completion of my throw.

Most knife throwers point the non-throwing arm at the target. I don't. As a carryover from my stick-fighting training, I keep my non-throwing arm in front of my chest or at my side.

SWING BACK AND INHALE

Swing your arm back. At the same time, shift your body weight from your front to your rear foot. Inhale as you swing your arm back then hold your breath as you complete the movement. The backward swing should be smooth and not hurried.

In the overhand throw, do not pull your arm too far back, as this will cause your body to tilt backward. This will result in a subsequent forward motion that will be more like pushing the knife rather than throwing it. Merely twist your body as you pull your arm back.

In the underhand throw, swing your arm back like a pendulum. Do not swing the ax past the height of your hips. As a rule, stop your backward swing when you start feeling uncomfortable.

END OF THE BACKWARD SWING

For a knife that is a lot lighter than an ax, there is a momentary pause at the end of the backward swing. I throw a light ax overhand in the same way.

To throw a heavy ax, I swing my arm like a pendulum backward and downward at the side of my body. In a continuous counterclockwise circular motion, I bring it up above my shoulder, after which I start my forward swing. Because the ¼" VCM Palakol weighs over a pound, I cannot allow it to come to a dead stop. Hence, with the continuous circular backward then forward swing, I "slingshot" the ax toward the target (Figure 16).

FORWARD SWING AND HOLDING THE BREATH

The forward swing should be smooth. At the same time, you have to hold your breath. As the forward swing progresses, the weight of the body shifts to the front foot.

In the overhand throw, there is a slight swishing sound (as your arm and knife cut the air) toward the end of the forward swing and at the time of release. In the underhand throw, the arm swings forward like a pendulum.

RELEASE AND EXHALE

The knife must be held with just the right amount of "squeeze." If held too lightly, it will release early. If held too tightly, it will release late.

In the overhand throw, a premature release will cause the knife to sail over the target; a late release will cause the knife to hit the foot of the target. The reverse will result from early and late releases in the underhand throw.

The release of the knife must be by the "feel" imprinted on your subconscious through hundreds or thousands of throws. Indeed, the knife will release itself. The momentum of the knife will make it pull away on a tangent from the circular arc that your arm traces in its forward swing.

The release of the knife must be simultaneous with the completion of the shift of your body weight to the front foot and your exhale. You could liken the exhale to the kiai in karate or to the grunt in weightlifting. However, my exhale at the end of the knife throw is not as loud.

Do not cut your forward swing short. The eyes must stay focused on the target until seconds after the knife hits.

In the overhand throw, the right (or left) hand should end at the height of the hip. In the underhand throw, the right (or left) hand should end at the height of the shoulder.

I place my (empty) left hand in front of my chest or at my side at the start of my right-hand throw. However, as the forward swing progresses, I swing my left hand backward to effect a powerful throw and keep my balance.

FACTORS THAT AFFECT THE MECHANICS OF THE THROW

The design of the handle will affect the timing of the release when you throw a knife by its handle. For example, a flared, knobbed, or long handle will delay the release. On the other hand, a tapered handle will speed up the release. A ventilated handle will provide a desirable drag and will enable the knife to stay longer in the hand.

In a blade throw, the design of the blade will also affect the timing of the release. You will tend to release a narrow-bladed double-edged knife or a single-edged knife with a serrated back early. Nicks in your knife will make you open up your fingers prematurely.

Be aware of details around you that will affect the mechanics of your swing. For example, baggy pants or an unzipped jacket will hinder your underhand forward swing, particularly on a windy day. Worse, if your elbow is bent too much, your knife could get caught in your jacket pocket. Even in the overhand throw, a flapping jacket will affect your forward swing.

Several other factors will affect the mechanics of your throw. These include:

1. environmental conditions (sun, wind, temperature, bugs)
2. fatigue
3. mental clutter, such as fear of not sticking or of damaging the knife
4. emotional stress
5. trying too hard
6. condition of your eyes

A.

B.

C.

D.

FIGURE 11.

The forward motion and follow-through in the right-hand overhand throw from over the right shoulder (A-B-C). If the knife is not released, the forward motion becomes a knife cut (A-B-D).

A.

B.

C.

D.

FIGURE 12.

The forward motion and follow-through in the right-hand underhand throw from beside the right leg (A-B-C). If the knife is not released, the forward motion becomes a knife cut (A-B-D).

A.

B.

C.

FIGURE 13.

The forward motion and the follow-through in the right-hand overhand throw from over the left shoulder.

A.

B.

FIGURE 14.

The forward motion and the follow-through in the right-hand underhand throw from beside the left hip.

A.

B.

C.

D.

FIGURE 15.

The windup in the right-hand overhand throw that I use on the ³⁄₁₆" thick VCM Palakol. The follow-through is the same as that for the throwing of a knife.

A.

B.

C.

D.

Figure 16.

The windup in the right-hand overhand throw that I use on the heavier ¼" VCM Palakol. The follow-through is the same as that for the throwing of a knife.

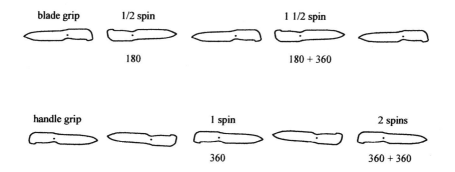

blade grip   1/2 spin   1 1/2 spin

180   180 + 360

handle grip   1 spin   2 spins

360   360 + 360

FIGURE 17.

For a knife to stick to the target, it must make half spins when thrown in the blade grip and full spins when thrown in the handle grip. In contrast, the two-pointed bagakay will stick whether it makes full (1, 2, . . .) or half ($\frac{1}{2}$, $1\frac{1}{2}$, . . .) spins. Note that this diagram is not intended to indicate the knife's trajectory.

SPINS AND ROTATIONS

As soon as you release the knife (or any throwing implement), it will spin end over end around its center of gravity (CG) toward the target. If the knife is to stick, you must control its rotation and spin such that it will hit the target point first. But how do you control the spin and the rotation of a knife?

SPIN

You would have achieved control if the knife reaches the target point first after it spins 180° (half spin), 360° (one spin), 360° + 180° (1½ spin), and so on. Of course, depending on how you hold the knife and the distance you are throwing from, the knife might make the ½, 1, or 1½ spins and yet hit butt first. See Figure 17.

At this point, let me make a distinction between the spin and the rotation of the knife. Spin is defined in reference to the tip of the knife. Rotation on the other hand is in reference to the CG of the knife.

Several factors will determine the rate at which the knife will spin.

1. Bend in the wrist. There is a right time and a wrong time to bend the wrist. The right time is *after* the elbow has been straightened to the maximum comfortable limit. Bending the

wrist at any other time will result in inconsistent if not inaccurate throws.

2. Relative distance of the index finger or thumb from the CG of the knife. The farther the CG of the knife is from the tip of your index finger, the faster the knife will spin. Thus, the ax thrown underhand gripped with the thumb about two inches from its CG (Figure 27B) will spin faster than the ax thrown underhand gripped with the thumb at its CG (Figure 27C).

3. Design of the handle. The knob of the handle of a knife such as the VM Bulalakaw (Figure 18, top) can catch on the heel of the palm or on the finger thereby creating a more pronounced spin. This will not happen if the knife has a smooth handle such as the CM Bituin (Figure 18, bottom).

Any knife or ax will spin clockwise if thrown overhand (Figures 19, 21); counterclockwise (Figures 20, 22) if thrown underhand. However, if the target is very close, it will seem not to. The knife could hit the target before its spin becomes noticeable.

The spin of some throwing implements can be suppressed but only at close distances. For example, I am able to suppress the spin of the Chinese flying dart when throwing it from 17 feet. I am able to do the same with the Japanese negishi-ryu shuriken when throwing it from 18 feet.

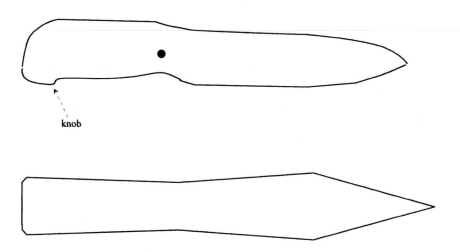

knob

FIGURE 18.

The knob of the VM Bulalakaw (top) will catch on the heel of the palm, and that will give it a more pronounced spin than if a knife has a smooth handle (bottom).

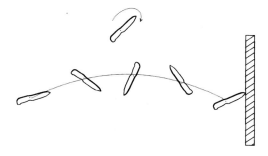

FIGURE 19.

A knife will spin clockwise (viewed from the right side of the knife thrower) when thrown overhand.

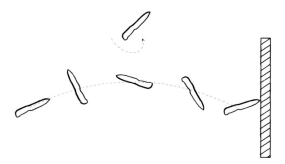

FIGURE 20.

A knife will spin counterclockwise (viewed from the right side of the knife thrower) when thrown underhand.

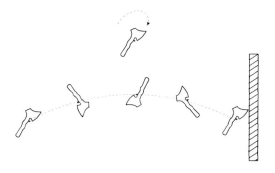

FIGURE 21.

An ax will spin clockwise (viewed from the right side of the ax thrower) when thrown overhand. This spin is transmitted to the ax by the clockwise rotation of the arm.

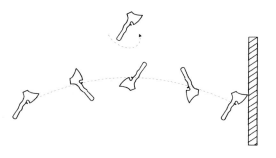

FIGURE 22.

An ax will spin counterclockwise (viewed from the right side of the ax thrower) when thrown underhand. This spin is transmitted to the ax by the counterclockwise rotation of the arm.

Heavy knives such as the Bowie can also be thrown underhand by the handle with "no" spin. The knife is simply shoveled toward the target. The "no" spin throw is ideal at point-blank range.

It is easier to leave the spin of the knife to the laws of physics. Instead of trying to control it, adjust to it. Step back to allow the knife to spin a few more degrees, or move forward to make the knife stick on the target before it spins a few more degrees.

The spins and rotations of other throwing implements are discussed and illustrated in later sections.

It is not necessary to know the number of spins a throwing implement makes to stick to the target. It can become mental clutter. For example: I throw with my right and left hands using different grips and different implements from different distances; I do not want to clutter my brain with the number of spins my knife makes for each of my throws. I do not have to know this when I throw my knife. When I teach, I do not tell my students to make the knife spin ½, 1, 1½ times and so on. I merely tell them to either move back or step forward several inches at a time. Or, to give the knife a little more or a little less spin.

I make the beginning student throw (using the blade grip) from a distance such that the knife will make half spins because that way he can see how the knife will hit the target. Hence, it will be easier for him to make corrections on the throw. If a beginning knife thrower throws a knife with 1½ spins, he will not see how it impacts and will not be able to make corrections if it does not stick. Of course, if you do not have a teacher, you can ask a friend to observe how the knife hits.

ROTATION

The thrown knife will rotate around three mutually perpendicular axes: longitudinal, medial and transverse (Figure 23). The design of its handle, the grip used, and the method of throwing will determine which rotation is more noticeable.

While the thrown knife can be made to rotate around any one of its axes, there is no such option with an ax. The ax will have to be made to rotate at its CG (Figure 24) around its medial axis (Figure 25). Otherwise, the result of the throw will be unpredictable.

MEDIAL AXIS. The VM Bulalakaw or any knife thrown overhand by the handle in the curled finger blade grip (Figure 26A) or by the blade in the straight finger blade grip (Figure 26B) will rotate most noticeably on its medial axis and will have minimal rotation on the longitudinal axis.

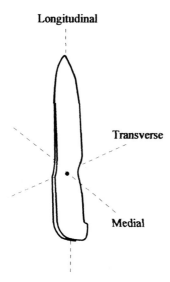

Longitudinal

Transverse

Medial

FIGURE 23.

A thrown knife will rotate about its CG (shown as a dot) along three axes: longitudinal, medial, and transverse.

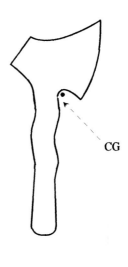

CG

FIGURE 24.

The CG of the VCM Palakol, shown as a dot (.), is outside its body.

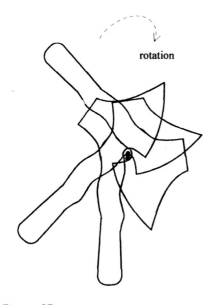

rotation

FIGURE 25.

For an ax to stay on a true course, it has to rotate around its medial axis. This shows an ax rotating (on a plane parallel to the paper) around its medial axis.

The VM Bulalakaw, which has a nonsymmetrical handle, when thrown underhand by the handle using the curled finger handle grip (Figure 26C) with the flat of its blade facing the ground can be made to rotate around its medial axis. The medial axis rotation is possible because as the knife is released the knob of the handle catches on the heel of the palm while the tapered top slides off smoothly.

A knife with a symmetrical handle, such as the CM Bituin, if thrown overhand by the handle using the curled finger handle grip (Figure 26D), will slide smoothly off the palm with neither the top nor the bottom part of the handle catching. Thrown in this manner the CM Bituin can be made to rotate around its medial axis.

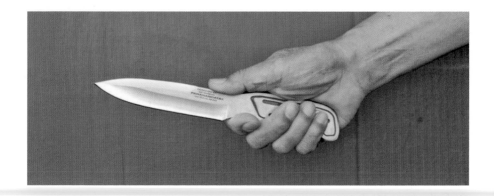

A. Curled finger handle grip in the overhand throw used on the VM Bulalakaw.

B. Straight finger blade grip in the overhand throw used on the VM Bulalakaw.

C. Curled finger handle grip in the underhand throw used on the VM Bulalakaw.

D. Curled finger handle grip in the overhand throw used on the CM Bituin.

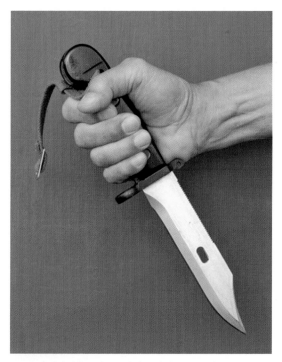

FIGURE 26.

Medial axis rotation. A knife can be made to rotate around its medial axis by using these grips. (A gymnast who cartwheels rotates around the medial axis.) The ice-pick grip can be used effectively only on a flat- and thick-handled knife such as the AK-47 bayonet. The ice-pick grip, used on a thin-handled knife, can only lead to inconsistent if not bad throws.

E. Ice-pick hold in the underhand throw used on an AK-47 bayonet.

The AK-47 bayonet will rotate around its medial axis when thrown underhand using the ice-pick hold (Figure 26E). Its weight and its thick handle will make it easy to throw the bayonet with little wobble.

It is neither logical nor practical to attempt to throw the VCM Palakol or any ax using any other grip than the curled finger handle grip (Figure 27). This

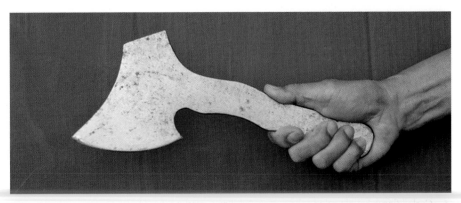

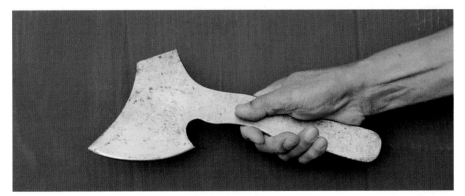

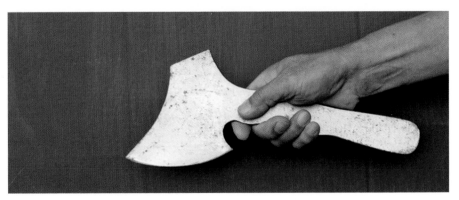

C.

FIGURE 27.

Medial axis rotation. An ax can be made to rotate around its medial axis by using this grip. Any wobble (rotation of an ax in its transverse axis) will result in inconsistent and inaccurate throws.

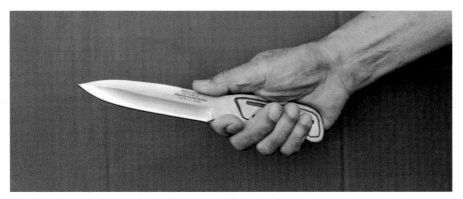

A. Curled finger handle grip in the underhand throw used on the VM Bulalakaw.

B. Wraparound handle grip (forward hold) in the underhand throw used on an AK-47 bayonet.

FIGURE 28.

Longitudinal axis rotation. An knife can be made to rotate around its longitudinal axis by using these grips and turning the hand slightly over at the time of release. (A properly thrown football will rotate around its longitudinal axis. A figure skater's triple loop is a rotation around the longitudinal axis.) The wraparound handle grip can be used on either a thin- or thick-handled knife.

is the only grip that can be used to throw the ax to make it rotate about its medial axis. Consider yourself lucky if you are able to make a wobbly ax stick to the target.

LONGITUDINAL AXIS. The VM Bulalakaw can be made to rotate around its longitudinal axis when thrown underhand using the curled finger handle grip (Figure 28A). At the time of release, I turn my hand over slightly to give the VM Bulalakaw a pronounced longitudinal axis rotation.

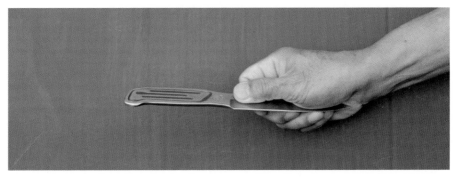

A. Curled finger blade grip in the overhand or underhand throw used on the VM Bulalakaw.

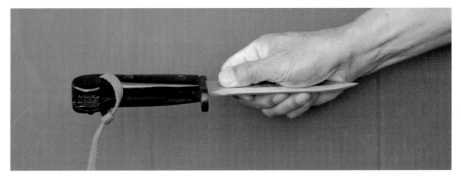

B. Curled finger blade grip in the underhand throw used on the AK-47 bayonet.

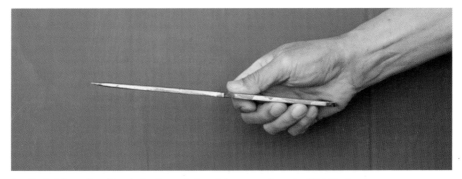

C. Curled finger handle grip in the underhand throw used on the CM Bituin.

FIGURE 29.

Transverse axis rotation. A knife can be made to rotate around its transverse axis by using the curled finger grip. (A gymnast who somersaults rotates around his transverse axis.)

Similarly, the CM Bituin can be made to rotate on a pronounced longitudinal axis when thrown using the curled finger handle grip, by turning the hand over slightly at the time of release. The result is quite dramatic. The CM Bituin or any knife thrown in such a manner will corkscrew on its way to the target.

TRANSVERSE AXIS. A knife such as the CM Bituin, VM Bulalakaw, or AK-47 bayonet can be made to rotate on its transverse axis using the curled finger handle grip.

This grip can be used either on the blade (Figure 29A, Figure 29B) or on the handle (Figure 29C). Here, the knife is held with the flat of its blade facing the ground.

If you are able to give a knife a marked transverse axis rotation, it will head toward its target as though in slow motion.

CASE STUDIES

I have studied the rotations and spins of the bagakay, the AK-47 bayonet, and the VCM Palakol. Their different shapes make them interesting case studies in rotation and spin.

BAGAKAY. The cigar-shaped steel bagakay is a better throwing implement than a knife. Being two-pointed, it gives the thrower confidence that he can stick it. Hence, he can concentrate more on learning the mechanics of the throw rather than on worrying about hitting the target with the butt as is the case with a knife. After you become comfortable with the mechanics of the throw, learning to throw a knife will come easier.

The number of spins the 12¾" bagakay makes from different throwing distances using the grip as shown in Figure 49B are listed in Table 1.

TABLE 1. Spins of the bagakay.

Number of Spins	Distance, feet
1	13
2	23
3	33.5

To identify which end of the bagakay sticks, I wrap a narrow strip of orange electrical tape on one end. I also wrap colored tape around its middle for easy location on grass.

AK-47 BAYONET. The AK-47 bayonet was not designed to be thrown. However, it has excellent throwing characteristics. It is a versatile throwing weapon and can be thrown underhand and overhand using different grips on the handle and on the blade.

It is also sturdy. I have thrown each of the several used AK-47 bayonets I own more than 1,000 times, and there is still no movement in their bolsters. They were still as good as before. In contrast, the bolster of one other army-type knife became loose after only a hundred throws.

The most noticeable rotations of the AK-47 bayonet, using different grips, are summarized in Table 2. You can experiment with your throwing knife and generate a similar table.

TABLE 2. Rotations of the AK-47 bayonet.

Kind of Throw	Grip	Most Noticeable Rotation Axis
Underhand	Curled finger, handle	Medial
Underhand	Curled finger, blade	Transverse
Overhand	Straight finger, blade	Medial
Underhand	Forward hold, handle	Longitudinal
Underhand	Ice-pick hold, handle	Medial

VCM PALAKOL. The VCM Palakol or any ax can only be thrown correctly by making it rotate about its medial axis.

I have thrown the ¼" thick VCM Palakol as well as a lighter ³⁄₁₆" thick version both underhand and overhand using different placements of my thumb and index finger on its handle.

TABLE 3. Spins of the VCM Palakol thrown underhand and overhand.

Kind of Throw	Curled Finger Handle Grip	Number of Spins	Distance, in feet
Overhand	Figure 66	1	21½
Underhand	Figure 67	1	24

THROWING AND STICKING DISTANCES

For a knife or ax to stick to the target, it should be released from a given distance. This distance is called the *sticking distance*. This is to be differentiated from the distance of your front or rear foot to the target. It is important to know the difference.

The *throwing distance* is the distance from the tip of the toe of the lead foot to the target. The sticking distance is from the point of release of the knife to the target. Hence, the throwing distance is measured with respect to the foot while the sticking distance is measured with respect to the hand. The throwing distance is dependent on the length of the thrower's arm; sticking distance is not. To understand the difference more easily, consider two knife throwers: A who is 5'6" tall, and B who is 6'4". Each throws identical knives using the same blade grip.

A is able to stick her knife from a throwing distance of 18 feet with her knife making a full spin. With the given length of A's arm, she releases her knife at 16 feet. If 6'4" B throws the identical knife from 18 feet, he will not be able to make it stick. It will get to the target too soon. To make his knife stick, he has to move back because he has a longer arm.

Aside from the length of the arm, other factors could affect the throwing distance. These include:

1. Length of the knife. My throwing distance for a 6⅛" knife using the straight finger blade grip is 17½ feet. If I throw a 10" knife of identical design, I will have to move back several inches to make it stick. If I do not want to move back, I have to adjust my grip on the knife or make adjustments in my throw.
2. Method of throwing. My throwing distance using identical grips on the VCM Palakol in an overhand throw is 21½ feet; in an underhand throw, 24 feet.
3. Kind of grip used. My overhand throwing distance for the 8¾" VM Bulalakaw using the straight finger blade grip is about 17½ feet; using the curled finger blade grip, 22 feet.

If you do not yet know your throwing distance for a particular throw, grip, or knife, begin by throwing your knife from a range of 17 to 24 feet. If you are tall, start your throw from 24 feet. As you try to find your throwing distance, move half a foot at a time.

To find your throwing distance, observe how your knife hits the target. Point up? Point down? With the butt? Flat? Or just right? Figures 30 and 31 show

Angle of Impact	Overhand Throw	Underhand Throw
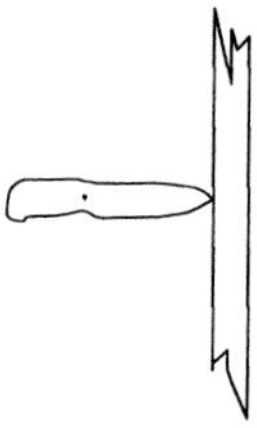 The knife hits perpendicular to the target.	Stay where you are.	Stay where you are.
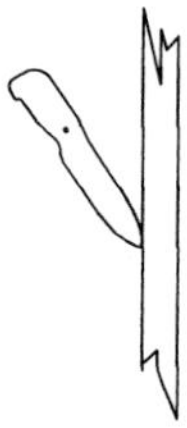 The knife hits with its tip down.	Step forward.	Step back.
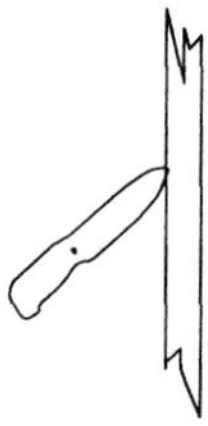 The knife hits with its tip up.	Step back.	Step forward.

FIGURE 30.

Finding your throwing distance for overhand and underhand knife throws.
When you make corrections, do not take big steps. Step forward or back a few inches at a time.

Overhand Throw	Distance Correction	Underhand Throw
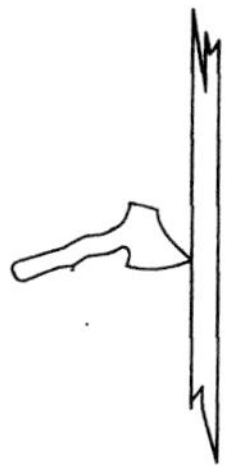 Tip of ax and its CG form a line that is perpendicular to the target face.	Stay where you are. Throwing distance is correct.	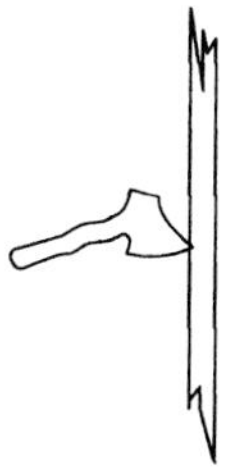 Tip of ax and its CG form a line that is perpendicular to the target face.
 Tip of ax points down.	Move closer to prevent the ax from over-rotating.	 Tip of ax points up.
 Tip of ax points down.	Move back to allow the ax to rotate a few more degrees.	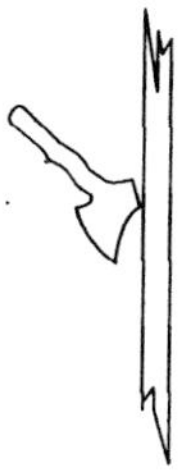 Tip of ax points down.

FIGURE 31.

Finding your throwing distance for overhand and underhand ax throws. When you make corrections, do not take big steps. Step forward or back a few inches at a time.

FIGURE 32.

The VCM Palakol and the VM Bulalakaw embedded on a cardboard target that is backed by plywood.

the possible orientations of the knife (ax) and how to make corrections to find your throwing distance. If your knife (ax) hits with its butt, you can either step forward or step back.

Once you are able to determine your throwing distance for a particular knife (ax) using a particular grip and a particular throw, mark it by driving a short visible stake into or by drawing a line on the ground. From here on, you should be able to stick your knife (ax) with accuracy and consistency (Figure 32).

INCREASING YOUR THROWING DISTANCE

After being able to stick your knife consistently and accurately from a given distance using a particular grip, throw, and knife, you might want to throw from farther away. How do you determine the next farther distance?

You can use trial and error as you did when you were just starting to learn how to throw and start scratching your head all over again, or you can use a little algebra.

Recall earlier that I made a distinction between sticking distance and throwing distance. They are related by the equation

Throwing distance = Sticking distance + Arm reach

FIGURE 33.

Relationship between throwing and sticking distances. Arm reach is the distance between your front toe and the point of contact with the ground of a plumb line dropped from the tip of your index finger.

This relationship is shown in Figure 33.

Arm reach will vary from one thrower to another. A thrower with longer arms will have a longer arm reach than one who has shorter arms.

A thrower's arm reach will become a constant, or nearly so, after the mechanics of a throw are committed to his neuromuscular memory (after many years of dedicated practice and thousands of throws). However, note that the thrower will stretch more to the front if the implement he is throwing is too heavy for him.

We can determine the next farther distance for a throw separately for blade and handle throws. The following calculations are based on a one-pointed knife—one with its center of gravity in the middle—thrown with a spin.

HANDLE THROW. The knife can be thrown by the handle at point-blank range or shoveled at the target from some distance with apparently no spin. However, from a farther distance, the knife will spin before it hits the target.

The knife has to make full spins (1, 2, 3,. . .) if it is to stick on the target when thrown by the handle (Figure 17, bottom). Obviously, the closest distance you can be to the target in order for the thrown knife to stick in the handle throw is when it makes one full spin. We will call this your *first* throwing distance (Figure 34). We will assign the value X feet to your sticking distance. Thus,

$$\text{First throwing distance} = X + \text{Arm reach} \qquad \text{(Equation 1)}$$

To determine your arm reach, drop a straight line from your fingertips at the point you release your knife; then measure the distance to the tip of your front toe. Arm reach will normally be about 1½ to 2 feet. We will use the lower value.

If you are able to make your knife stick from a throwing distance of 17 feet, your sticking distance is 17 - 1.5 = 15.5 feet. So X = 15.5 feet.

Your next (second) farther throwing distance for the handle throw will be 2X + 1.5 or

$$\text{Next (second) throwing distance} = 2(15.5) + 1.5 = 32.5 \text{ feet}$$

Hence, for the handle throw, Equation 1 becomes

$$\text{Throwing distance} = nX + \text{Arm reach} \qquad \text{(Equation 2)}$$

where n = 1, 2, 3 ,. . . full spins or n = first, second, third, . . . throwing distance. The quantity nX is the sticking distance.

Spin can be suppressed if the implement is gripped with its CG in the palm. For example, I am able to throw the 5 ⅝" negishi-ryu shuriken from 18 feet gripped with its point initially toward the target and make it stick with no spin. With this method of throwing, the shuriken behaves like a spear. I also use the no spin throw on the Chinese flying dart.

BLADE THROW. The knife has to make half spins (½, 1½, 2½, 3½, . . .) if it is to stick when thrown by the blade (Figure 17, top). Obviously, the closest distance you can be to the target in order for you to make the knife stick in a blade throw is when it makes one half spin. We will call this your *first* throwing distance (Figure 35). We will assign the value Z feet to your sticking distance and 1.5 feet to your arm reach:

$$\text{First throwing distance} = Z + 1.5$$

where Z is the distance needed to allow the knife to make ½ spin.

We will assume at this point that you are able to make your knife stick using the blade throw from 17 feet. This will make your blade throw sticking distance,

$$Z = 17 - 1.5 = 15.5 \text{ feet}$$

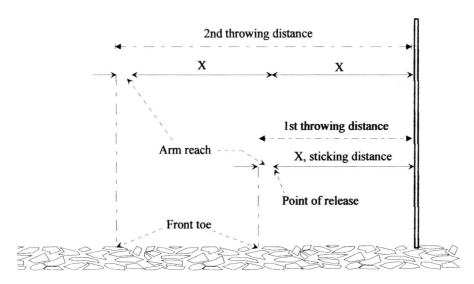

FIGURE 34.

Throwing distances for the handle throw.

After the first one half spin, the knife will hit the target point first. If the knife is allowed to make another one half spin and there is a target at that point, it will hit butt first—not the desired result. So, if the knife is to stick from farther away, your next (second) throwing distance should allow the knife to make a third half spin. Thus, for the blade throw, your

$$\text{Next (second) throwing distance} = Z + 2Z + 1.5 \text{ or}$$

$$\text{Next (second) throwing distance} = 3Z + 1.5$$

In our particular example, your

$$\text{Next (second) throwing distance} = 3(15.5) + 1.5 = 48 \text{ feet}$$

which could be a bit too far for you; you will need to walk 96 feet to throw and retrieve your knife, which is good if you want to lose weight or could use the exercise.

In general, for the blade throw

$$\text{Throwing distance} = (2n + 1)Z + \text{Arm reach} \qquad \text{(Equation 3)}$$

where $(2n + 1)$ is the number of half spins and $n = 0, 1, 2, 3, \ldots$ The quantity $(2n + 1)Z$ is the sticking distance.

Your first throwing distance for the blade throw is when $n = 0$. In our example, when $n = 2$, you will have to throw from 79 feet.

You might try to get around these algebraic equations and shorten the distance of your knife throws by bending your wrist before your elbow reaches its maximum comfortable extension. Don't. This will result in inconsistent and inaccurate throws such that in one throw your knife could hit point first; in the next, it could hit butt first. Or it could hit flat.

A story about a bayonet throw during World War II as narrated by author Harry K. McEvoy gives us an interesting opportunity to use the throwing distance calculations.

Skeeter Vaughan was at the head of a 6-man patrol of the Moccasin Rangers assigned to take a German pillbox. But first, they needed to eliminate the sentry. Although it was already dark, their uniform could give them away because of snow on the ground.

Skeeter Vaughan was a full blooded Cherokee from California. Because of his great skill, he became a professional knife thrower when still a teenager. Hence, he was asked by his men to take out the sentry. He threw a 16" bayonet

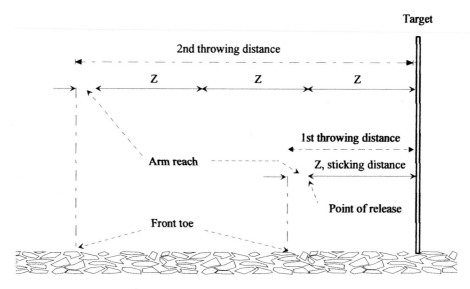

FIGURE 35.

Throwing distances for the blade throw

downhill, in the dark, and hit the German sentry on the base of the skull. The next morning the distance of the throw was measured. It was found to be 87 feet.*

I have assumed that the slope is 15 degrees, giving a horizontal throwing distance of about 85 feet. He used the blade throw. Most professional knife throwers throw from about 9 feet. At 5'8", his arm reach would be about 2 feet. It would be reasonable to assume a sticking distance of 9 feet because his bayonet is 16".

We can calculate the number of spins his bayonet made using Equation 3 for the blade throw. It came out to be 9 half spins or 4½ full spins. That was some throw!

TARGETS

You will need a good target set up in a location where there will be minimum risk of injury to you or other people. If possible, locate your outdoor target so you can throw in the shade during summer.

When throwing indoors, damage to floors can be minimized by covering them with cardboard. You may want to top the cardboard with used carpet.

Avoid throwing knives that weigh more than 6 ounces indoors. Do not throw axes indoors.

TYPE OF MATERIAL

STYROFOAM. You have a number of choices for your targets. You can try the Styrofoam target used in archery. This target is inexpensive if you throw only occasionally and if you use small, light knives. However, if you throw a lot, this target will quickly put a hole in your wallet. Also, if you throw heavy knives such as the AK-47 bayonet, you will use up the Styrofoam target in no time at all. Replacing Styrofoam targets gets even more expensive when you throw the much heavier ax.

WOOD. You can use wood for your target. It is relatively inexpensive. But, of course, the longevity of your wood target will still depend on the weights of the knives or axes you throw and also on how often and how many times you throw.

---

* Harry K. McEvoy, *Knife & Tomahawk Throwing*, pp. 88–93, 1988,
Charles E. Tuttle Company, Inc., Rutland, Vermont.

Throwing knives is normally a safe pastime. However, when your knife hits a wood target at an oblique angle, it can take a wild bounce, and you may be hit by the bouncing knife. In a garage or basement with limited room, it will not be easy to dodge such a projectile.

Even with your wood target set up outdoors, the possibility of getting hit by a bouncing knife still exists.

CARDBOARD. Cardboard is the ideal target if you throw knives indoors.

Cardboard sops up the energy of a badly thrown knife and causes the knife to fall harmlessly to the floor. Besides protecting your person, you will avoid breaking glass windows, mirrors, lights, or utility meters. Even outdoors, cardboard makes an ideal target.

I use cardboard in my backyard for a number of reasons. First, it does not cost anything. You can get it for free from your neighborhood stores. Second, the orientation of the knife (ax) gives me an idea of how the knife (ax) turned in flight. This is because dents caused by knife impacts, even if the knife does not stick, are visible on the cardboard, as would not have been the case with a wooden target. There you have to guess how the knife hit in order to find your throwing distance. This aspect of cardboard is particularly helpful when you are trying out a new throw. Third, the noise of a badly thrown knife (ax) is not a good thing to hear on a beautiful sunny afternoon when your neighbors are relaxing on their lawns.

I throw at least 300 times every day. If I make ten bad throws, that is ten knife-to-target impacts that I do not want to disturb my neighbors with. Even the knives that stick will generate dull thuds that can be bothersome to people who might not share your enthusiasm for throwing, so be aware of the impact your pastime can have on others nearby.

PREPARING THE TARGET

MOUNTING THE TARGET. The setup need not be elaborate. Figure 36 shows the dimensions and relative distances of the target support I use for my knife throws. The installed target is 6 feet tall (Figure 39) and costs less than $40. For this setup, you need two 4" x 3½" x 8' sections of landscape timber and six ½" x 3" x 4' sections of oak (or any hard wood).

Cut the landscape timber into 4-foot sections. Nail one ½" x 3" x 4' oak section on each side of the timber with a 1-foot overlap.

Dig three 1-foot-deep holes in the ground. Set the 4-foot sections in the holes then fill the holes with dirt. Use a tamper to compress the dirt. (There will be considerable movement of the timber when the soil becomes loose from rain.)

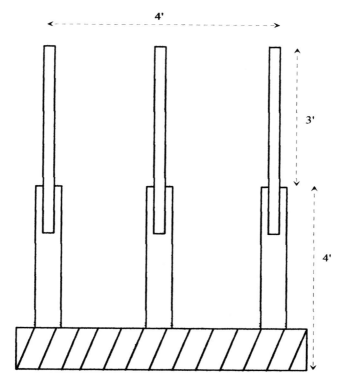

FIGURE 36.

Dimensions and relative distances of the target support for my knife throws. I use a different setup for my ax throws (Figure 37, Figure 38).

Attach the cardboard targets to the ½" x 3" x 4' wood using carpenter's clips. Use 4 or five layers of cardboard. You now have back-to-back targets.

You need back-to-back targets if you throw on grass. When the grass on one side thins, throw on the other side to give the thinned grass a chance to grow again.

The ¼" ax that I designed and fabricated weighs about a pound. Because it is heavy, it can easily put a big hole through several layers of cardboard. This will entail replacing the cardboard frequently. Indeed, after twenty ax throws, I have to replace the top cardboard because it gets mutilated. To somewhat reduce the size of the holes and to make the target last a few more throws, I use plywood as backing for at least eight layers of cardboard. The installed target (Figure 40) costs under $50.

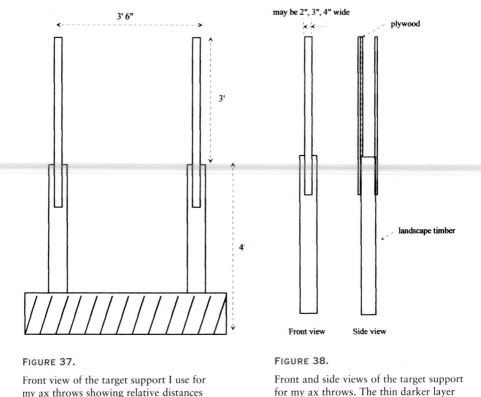

FIGURE 37.

Front view of the target support I use for my ax throws showing relative distances and dimensions.

FIGURE 38.

Front and side views of the target support for my ax throws. The thin darker layer is a section of plywood ($1^5/_{32}$" thick, 44" wide, 36" high) to which I clip at least eight layers of cardboard.

SIZE OF THE TARGET. When a knife is already embedded in the target, there is the possibility of the next thrown knife hitting it. If the knives you are throwing are all-metal, they will get nicked.

Knives with wood or plastic scales will suffer more damage. Their handles can get chipped or split by an incoming knife. This is very likely with knives such as the AK-47 bayonet, the handle of which is made of plastic that is $1^1/_8$" at its thickest. The AK-47 bayonet is a relatively inexpensive knife—you can get a used one for under $20. Still, you want the AK-47 bayonet, or any knife you're throwing, to last as long as possible.

You will need a wide target to reduce the possibility of nicks and chips in your knives. Wide targets will allow you to throw several knives before there is

FIGURE 39.

Multiple targets for my knife throws mounted on the target support shown in Figure 36.

FIGURE 40.

Installed target for my ax throws. The untidy looking hole-riddled cardboard at the foot of the target helps prevent dirt from getting on axes that hit point first but bounce off. Such an arrangement is even more important when the ground is wet.

a need to retrieve the already-embedded ones. A wide target is even more essential if you are a beginning knife thrower or if you are trying a new throw.

For precision sport knife throwing, your target will necessarily be small. For example: I use a set of concentric circles (Figure 41A) printed on an 8 ½" x 11" sheet of white paper. For defensive knife throwing, my target is a human face (Figure 41B) printed on the same size paper. You can also use several sheets of 8 ½" x 11" paper on a wide field (Figure 42) to minimize the possibility of damage to your knives.

If you try to throw around the already embedded knife, you will start missing your target.

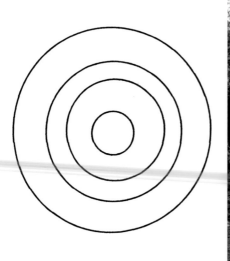

A.   B.

FIGURE 41.

For sport knife throwing, I aim at a set of concentric circles (A). For defensive knife throwing, I aim at an outline of a human face (B). I use carpenter's glue to paste them onto my cardboard backboards.

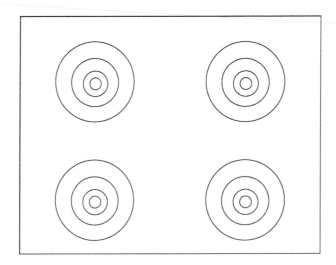

FIGURE 42.

Multiple targets to reduce the possibility of knife-to-knife impacts.

TRACKING YOUR PROGRESS
AND LEARNING CURVES

If you throw knives only occasionally, you might be satisfied with merely sticking your knife every now and then. However, if you take knife throwing as a serious sport, you will not be satisfied with a few sticks. You will want to stick your knife more often than you miss.

If you throw on a daily basis and want to keep track of your progress, you need to record your hits and misses. Otherwise, you will not remember if you had more sticks today than a week ago. You can keep track of your progress in a simple yet effective way. Just count the number of times your knife sticks to the target then divide this number by the total number of your throws. Multiply this number by 100 to give you your sticking percentage.

LEARNING CURVES

You can make the calculations and generate a graph of your sticking percentage manually, or you can use a computer. Using a computer worksheet, you can tabulate your sticking percentage and generate a graph. Figure 43 is such a graph and shows my sticking percentage for months 1, 4, 12, and 15 for my left-hand underhand throw using the handle grip.

The curve in month 1 is typical. I learned quickly, but I was erratic and inconsistent. I threw better in month 4, but I was still inconsistent. I had too many ups and downs; my hills were high and my valleys were deep. However, as I threw more (months 12 and 15), I was able to stick my knives more accurately and consistently. I still have peaks and valleys, but the variation is much smaller.

It is easier to keep track of your progress if you plot your *learning curve* after many more throws and over a longer period of time. For example: My learning curve for my left-hand underhand throw over a fifteen-month period is shown in Figure 44. This figure illustrates the typical shape of a learning curve. Learning comes quickly at first. For example, in the first month, the chart shows 57 percent sticks. This jumped to 70 percent in the following month. However, this rate of progress cannot continue indefinitely.

The learning curve is a limited growth curve—you cannot throw better than 100 percent. Eventually, you will reach the upper limit of your ability. For example, after month 11, my sticking percentage hovered in the low 90s. I still had a lot of room for improvement. However, I decided to learn other throws.

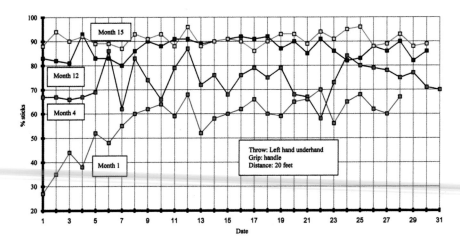

FIGURE 43.

A comparison of my left-hand underhand throw using the handle grip in four different months

I have recorded all my sticks and misses and generated the associated learning curves for all my throws. Some of these are shown in later sections and can be used as benchmarks against which you can compare your progress.

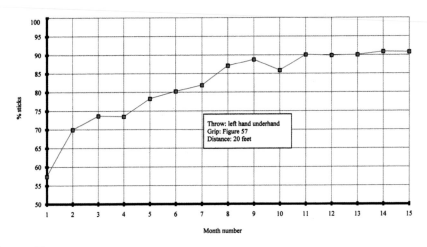

FIGURE 44.

My learning curve over a period of fifteen months for my left-hand underhand throw. I am right-handed.

I record the number of throws of my students. However, at their request, I do not record all their sticks and misses. In one such case, one of my students threw 2,400 times before she felt comfortable enough for me to start keeping track. Her learning curve is shown in Figure 45.

The curve is steep in the first three months. (It would appear still steeper if I had recorded the sticks and misses from the very first throw.) The steep portion of the learning curve I call the *frustration zone*. This is where a beginning knife thrower could give up in frustration not knowing what she/he is doing wrong. In my students' case, I watch them throw, give encouragement, and make corrections on throwing distance, the mechanics of the throw, the grip, or mental focus. If a student throws too fast or too hard, she/he has lost focus.

In the fourth month, this student got over the hump and started sticking in the mid-80s. From this month on, she progressed at a smooth pace. In the eleventh month, she hit a high of 93 percent. For some reason, in the twelfth and thirteenth month, her average dipped. I have experienced similar dips in my throwing averages over the years; it often is due to mental clutter.

On average, in about six months and after about 10,000 throws, your technique will become consistent and will begin to enjoy throwing knives.

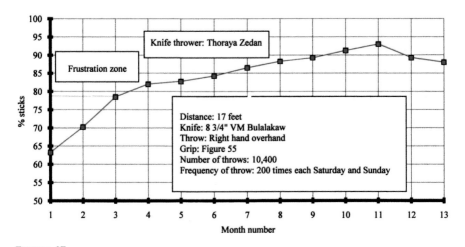

FIGURE 45.

Learning curve of one of my students. It takes about fifteen minutes to throw one hundred times, that is, if you have ten knives. If you have fewer, it will take longer.

Even after becoming skilled in throwing any implement, a number of factors will still affect your sticking average. These include:

1. Weight of throwing implement. For example, I am more accurate with a lighter ax than with a heavier one. I missed sticking the heavier ¼" thick ax 163 times out of 4,500 throws. I missed sticking the lighter ax 31 times out of 12,800 throws.
2. Distance of the throw. You become less accurate as you begin to throw from farther away.
3. Type of implement. For example, you may be more accurate when throwing an ax than when throwing a knife.
4. Throwing hand. You will notice a difference between your right-hand and left-hand throws.
5. Method of throwing. You will be more accurate with one method than with another in the beginning.
6. Type of grip. You may find that you are more accurate with the forward hold than with the ice-pick hold.

Other factors, such as loss of concentration could affect your sticking average. For instance, if you've already hit the target ninety-eight straight times, missing could cross your mind—and very likely you will miss. Lapses in concentration can also be caused by physical distractions.

Distractions could take the form of a passing cloud covering the sun, a gust of wind, a siren blaring, or a squirrel in your peripheral vision. These factors could cause your throw to go awry, and they are all reflected in the learning curves.

It is not that difficult to throw an implement ten times and score a perfect ten. However, it is many times more difficult to throw fifty times and score a perfect fifty. It is even more difficult to score a perfect one hundred. For these reasons, I recommend throwing the implements in sets of fifty or one hundred.

To illustrate the difficulty of consistent sticks, I tabulated the frequency with which I came close to scoring fifty (hitting the target forty-nine out of fifty throws) and scoring a perfect fifty throwing the Chinese flying sticker. Since I threw the stickers in sets of fifty, it was not a problem grouping two consecutive sets of fifty throws into one set of one hundred throws.

TABLE 4.

Frequency of perfect and almost-perfect scores for the flying sticker
(Range of scores: 30–50 hits)

Score	Frequency, Number of Times
49	137
50	112
99	34
100	23

Since I threw the flying sticker fifty times a day over a period of 390 days (13 months), I had 390 chances of scoring perfect 50s. However, I was able to do so only 112 times. Scoring a perfect 100 is even more difficult. I had 195 chances but was able to do so only 23 times.

- CHAPTER 2 -

MY THROWING IMPLEMENTS

All the throwing implements in this section are "mine" only because later in life I designed and fabricated them.

Many throwing implements are available in the market. However, I have chosen the bagakay (dart), VM Bulalakaw (knife), VCM Palakol (ax), and sibat (spear) to represent the most common throwing implements. Seemingly out of place in this section is the AK-47 bayonet, but because I throw it in a unique way, I have included it here.

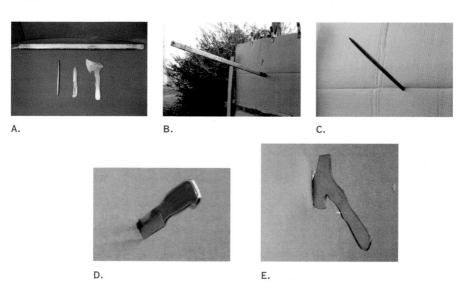

A.   B.   C.

D.   E.

FIGURE 46.

My throwing implements (A), spear (B), bagakay (C), VM Bulalakaw (D), and VCM Palakol (E) shown embedded on my cardboard target.

BAGAKAY

The bagakay was used by Filipinos to hunt birds for centuries before 1521, when the Philippines became a Spanish colony. There are historical accounts of the use of the bagakay to bring down birds from twenty paces (which is about thirty-five feet for the average-height Filipino) as well as its use against the Spanish colonists. In one instance of its use against the enemy, the bagakay was thrown with such violence that it pierced a Spanish soldier's armor and killed him.

The bagakay is a two-pointed (Figure 47) wooden dart. It can be made from hollow bamboo, which can be filled with clay to make it heavier and easier to

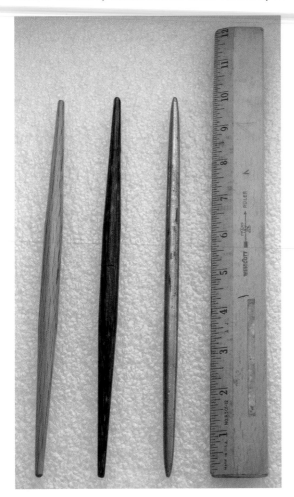

throw. Obviously, any small branch of a tree can also be cut to the proper length, then sharpened at both ends to become an impromptu bagakay. It can then be fire-hardened to keep its point longer.

The wooden bagakay is a good throwing weapon despite its lightness. The bagakay is cigar-shaped but much thinner. The obvious way to make one is with a lathe. But you can also make do with a belt sander.

I rough-shape bagakays with a file, then give them a final finish on a belt sander. I have made 10-inch bagakays from oak, *bahi* (a Philippine palm wood), and steel.

One 10-inch bagakay that I fabricated from bahi weighs a mere 19 grams (0.68 ounces).

FIGURE 47.

Two-pointed bagakays (l, r) made from oak, bahi, and steel.

Gripping a bagakay

A bagakay is two-pointed, so it does not matter which end is gripped. The two grips I use on the bagakay are shown in Figure 48. The straight finger blade grip (Figure 48A) has limited use in close-quarter fighting. The curled finger blade grip (Figure 48B) is the more practical grip. I use both grips to throw the bagakay, but I have better control when I use the curled finger blade grip.

Throwing a bagakay

Throw wooden bagakays overhand from over your right shoulder assuming you are right-handed. It requires a lot more effort to throw the light bagakay from over the left shoulder. I would advise against throwing a wooden bagakay underhand due to its lightness. I have thrown wooden bagakays from seventeen feet up to five at a time. So far, my best effort is to stick four out of five bagakays thrown simultaneously.

I throw the heavier steel bagakays from over my left and right shoulders, from beside my right leg and from beside my left hip.

The bagakay will stick on the target whether it makes half or full spins because it is two-pointed. However, the bagakay still has to be thrown from a given distance to make it stick.

Because bagakays are two-pointed, you cannot be too careful when you handle them. When you retrieve the bagakays, *first* pull out those that are embedded on the target. Any bagakays that fell on the ground should be retrieved *last*. This will prevent you from getting poked in the eye.

Learning curve case study

Throwing from 33 feet requires a lot of effort. If you have not thrown from this distance before, you might experience some soreness in your hip (opposite that of your throwing arm). However, the pain will go away in a couple of days.

A bagakay thrown from 33 feet has a lot of power and can split 1-inch thick wooden flooring material. Targets, if made of cardboard, must be at least eight layers thick.

KNIFE

Many throwing knives of different shapes, sizes, appearance, weights, and costs are available in the market. However, you will not find them all in one place.

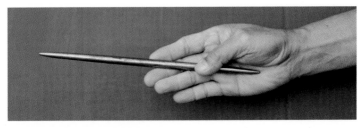

A. Straight finger blade grip.

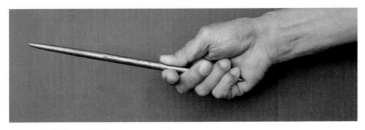

B. Curled finger blade grip.

FIGURE 48.

The grips I use on a bagakay.

Even if you find five throwing knives pictured in a catalog or displayed on a store shelf, you will need certain guidelines to make an intelligent choice as to which knife to buy.

SELECTING A KNIFE

An intelligent choice can be made based on feel—the knife's weight and location of its center of gravity (CG), appearance—the shape of the blade and handle, overall length, which is directly related to weight, and cost. The interplay of these factors will determine the knife's throwing characteristics. These are listed in Table 5.

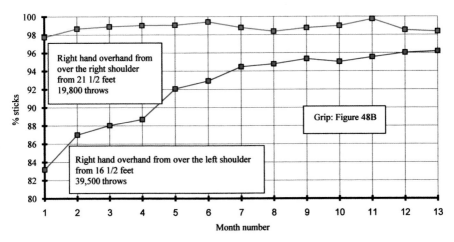

FIGURE 49.

My learning curve for throwing steel bagakays using the right-hand overhand throw from both the right and left shoulder

TABLE 5. Factors to consider in selecting a throwing knife

WEIGHT
BLADE DESIGN AND DIMENSION
shape – leaf, diamond, clip point, spearpoint
width – narrow, wide
edge – double, single, dull
HANDLE DESIGN AND DIMENSION
flat, thin, thick
contoured to fit palm
even, tapered, flared, knobbed
OVERALL LENGTH
COST

WEIGHT. A knife will throw well if it weighs at least 4 to 6 ounces. This weight is particularly suited to throwing indoors. If your indoor practice room has a low ceiling, you will be better off with a 6-ounce knife which you can throw underhand. However, these knives will still leave pockmarks even if the floor is protected by a couple of layers of cardboard or carpet.

Outdoors, even 4-ounce knives can be pushed far enough by a 25 mph cross-wind to cause you to miss your target. Of course, if you throw on grass or on bare ground, only your arm strength will limit the weight of the knife you can throw.

If you throw overhand, you will manage to make knives as light as 2 ounces stick on the target. But for the underhand throw, even 4-ounce knives are too light. Baseball, softball, and lacrosse players share the same experience. Consider Table 6.

Lacrosse and baseball use balls that weigh approximately 5 ounces. In both sports, the ball is thrown overhand. (In lacrosse, a pouched racket is used to hurl the ball.) Softball uses a heavier ball that weighs 6¼–7 ounces. The softball is thrown underhand. Thus, there is a certain universality of throwing experiences among lacrosse, baseball, and softball players on one hand and knife throwers on the other. Heavier knives, and balls, are easier to throw underhand than the lighter ones.

TABLE 6. Weights of sports balls and hockey pucks.

Sport Balls/Hockey Pucks	Weight, in ounces
Golf ball	1.62 max.
Handball	2.3
Tennis	2–2½
Lacrosse	5–5½
Field hockey	5½–5¾
Baseball	5–5¼
Ice hockey	6
Softball	6¼–7
Volleyball	9
Football	14–15
Soccer ball	14–18
Basketball	20–22

You cannot feel the weight of a knife unless you hold it in your hands, and if you are buying it from a catalog, this is not possible. However, you can use the dimensions of a knife to get an idea of how much it will weigh. For example: If a knife is 8 inches long and at least ⅛-inch thick, it will weigh at least four ounces. I have seen only one catalog that listed the weights of its throwing knives.

BLADE SHAPE AND DIMENSION. The shape of the blade (Figure 50A–D) will not make one knife a better thrower than another. However, it can determine the grip on the knife.

If the blade is wide enough and single-edged, it can be thrown by the blade. If the knife has a wide blade or is double-edged, it has to be thrown by the handle. Knives with wide blades can pop out of the target even after sticking.

Throwing knives that are diamond-shaped (Figure 50A) or leaf-shaped (Figure 50B) are usually dull. If a knife is double-edged, it can be dulled by filing or by grinding.

The VM Bulalakaw is one-edged and has a drop point (Figure 50C) that curves away from the heel of the palm. Hence, when thrown by the blade, there is little risk of the point cutting into the palm. A knife with a clip point (Figure 50D) can also be thrown by the blade. However, I prefer to throw any knife with a clip point by the handle.

HANDLE SHAPE AND DIMENSION. Handles (Figure 51) of throwing knives are designed to conform to the contour of the palm and to allow the same place-

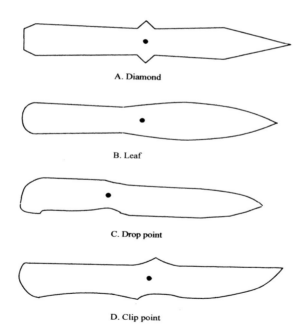

A. Diamond

B. Leaf

C. Drop point

D. Clip point

FIGURE 50.

Different shapes of blades of throwing knives that I designed. The dot is the location of the knife's CG. (This and all other sketches are not drawn to scale.)

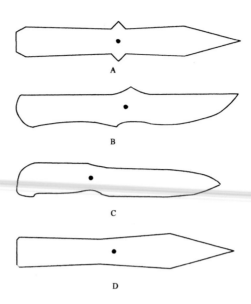

Figure 51.

Different shapes of handles of throwing knives that I designed. **A.** In-line hilt. **B.** Off-line hilt. **C.** Hilt-less. **D.** Hilt-less hourglass.

ment of the thumb and index finger from one throw to the next. For example: The in-line hilt (Figure 51A) and the off-line hilt (Figure 51B) allow the correct placement of the thumb and index finger for each throw. At the same time, the hilts serve as finger stops.

In contrast, the VM Bulalakaw (Figure 51C) is hilt-less. To ensure the correct grip, the thumb is placed on its sloping back at the same time that the little finger is pressed against its knob. The curved underside of its handle follows the contour of the closed palm.

It will seem that the handle of the hilt-less hourglass (Figure 51D) does not allow for consistent grips. It does. The knife's handle will press against the heel of the palm. At the same time, the thumb and index finger are correctly placed at its narrow waist.

Not only the shape but also the length and thickness of the handle and the material it is made of have to be considered in the selection of a knife. Throwing knives that are ⅛-inch thick could buckle when they make contact with a hard surface. The thicker ³⁄₁₆-inch knives can be thrown indefinitely without bending.

Avoid throwing knives that have wood or plastic scales since they can easily get damaged. Get all-metal throwing knives that have handles that are at least 4 inches long.

OVERALL LENGTH. It is easier to throw longer and heavier knives. A throwing knife with a 4-inch handle will have a total length of at least 8 inches. This is a good length for a throwing knife or for a knife designed for hand-to-hand combat.

COST. Most throwing knives are reasonably priced. A more expensive knife is not necessarily better for throwing. You would not want to nick an expensive knife. Any concern about a nick in your knife will become mental clutter and could cause your throw to err.

DESIGNING A KNIFE

A throwing knife must have heft. It must be heavy enough to feel good in the hands. A knife made of steel with the proper dimensions will give you the necessary heft. For example: A throwing knife made from a $3/16$-inch (thickness) by $1\frac{1}{8}$-inch (width) by 9 inches (length) steel plate will weigh about 244 grams or 8.7 ounces. The knife will weigh closer to 8 ounces because material will be removed to shape the handle and finished to give the knife a sharp edge. An 8-ounce knife will have enough heft and will stick with authority.

Obviously, if you want a heavier knife, you will either have to make it from a wider, longer or a thicker steel plate. However, a throwing knife can only be of a certain length and weight before it becomes impractical to carry it on your person.

I named my knife the VM Bulalakaw, VM to honor the memory of my father. When I was growing up, my father and I would look up at the moonlit night. From time to time we saw meteors. Bulalakaw, in my Philippine dialect, means meteor.

LENGTH OF THE HANDLE. Because I also teach the art of knife fighting, my goal was to design a knife that could be used for two requirements: throwing and fighting. My knife's handle had to allow for a quick release for knife throwing. At the same time, it also had to allow a secure grip for knife fighting. Unfortunately, these two factors are mutually exclusive.

I decided that this throwing knife must have a knob (Figure 52) to stop it from slipping through my fingers. The knob will not allow for a quick release. However, I rationalized that, if I wanted to give the knife a pronounced medial axis rotation, the knob is a desirable feature.

A knife must be fully in the grasp in hand-to-hand combat. Hence, including the knob, my knife has a 4-inch handle. (If you have big hands, the handle of your knife can be longer.)

I gave my knife a sloping back toward the front to ensure the same placement of the thumb for each throw. I also gave my knife a gradual downward slope at the back to give the heel of my palm a comfortable rest.

CENTER OF GRAVITY. I wanted the CG (Figure 50) of my knife to be, literally, at my fingertips. I located the CG of my knife in the handle to enable me to place my index finger (and thumb) over it in the handle throw. Thus, I decided that the CG of my knife must be at the 4-inch mark. I also wanted the CG to be close to the middle of the knife to enable me to place the tip of my index finger close to the CG in the blade throw.

LENGTH OF THE BLADE. A sharp knife will have a wedge-shaped blade. This will shave off some weight from the blade and will shift the knife's CG. To keep the CG where it is, the blade can be made a little longer than the handle, which will make the blade to handle length ratio slightly greater than one. A ratio of one means that the length of the blade is equal to the length of the handle.

The throwing knives that I have designed and fabricated have the following proportions.

$$1 < \frac{\text{blade length}}{\text{handle length}} < 1.24$$

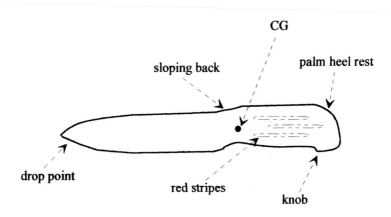

FIGURE 52.

One of the knives that I designed. The VM Bulalakaw has a sloping back that ensures the same placement of the thumb for each throw, a knob that stops it from slipping through the fingers, and a gradual down slope on the back of the handle that allows the heel of the palm to rest comfortably on it. An added feature, the three red stripes on its handle, makes it easy to locate the knife in grass.

A.

B.

C.

FIGURE 53.

Hand-to-hand combat grip. The VM Bulalakaw can be gripped in three different ways for hand-to-hand combat: with the thumb held on top of the handle (A) or with the fingers wrapped around the handle in the forward (B) and ice-pick (C) holds.

This means that the blade to handle length ratio is greater than one but less than 1.24. Using the higher ratio, with a handle length of 4 inches, the length of the blade would be 4.96 inches. This gives the knife a total length of 9 inches.

A cursory glance at knife catalogs, and some arithmetic, will show you that most of the smaller throwing knives have blade to handle length ratios of less than one. The longer throwing knives have ratios greater than one. Army-type knives such as the AK-47 bayonet and the K-Bar have ratios that are, respectively, 1.24 and 1.03.

You can compare this ratio to those of knives that are designed for cutting such as the *kukri* and the Philippines' *bolo*, which have long blades. Contrast this to folding knives where the handle is a lot longer than the blade.

Gripping a knife

A knife can be gripped and thrown by the blade or by the handle. Which grip should you learn first? It's up to you; it's simply a matter of personal preference, and of the knife's properties.

Most knives that have leaf- or diamond-shaped blades are two-edged and have to be gripped and thrown by the handle. Even one-edged knives with serrated backs have to be thrown by the handle. Otherwise, the serration will cut the skin raw after repeated throws.

The one other factor that will determine where a knife should be gripped is the location of its center of gravity (CG). You want to feel a certain "heft" in the knife. If the knife is handle-heavy (its CG is at its handle), you will have a tendency to grip and throw it by the blade. If it is blade-heavy (its CG is at its blade), which is the case for most double-edged throwing knives, it feels better to grip and throw the knife by the handle.

Blade grip. You will feel most comfortable using the blade grip when its point does not touch your wrist. At the same time, the CG of the knife must be no more than a couple of inches away from the tip of your thumb or index finger. The closer the CG of the knife is to the tip of your thumb or index finger, the easier it is to control its rotation and spin.

The knife can be held using the *curled finger blade grip* (Figure 54) where the thumb is placed on the flat of the blade with the tips of the other three big fingers on the opposite side. In this grip, the thumb is used as the pointer, and the knife is thrown with its flat facing the ground.

The knife can also be held in the *straight finger blade grip* (Figure 55) where the thumb is held extended over the top of the blade. All the other fingers are straight and point to the front. The flat of the blade rests on the index and middle fingers, and the index finger functions as the pointer. Held in this manner, the knife can be thrown with the flat of its blade on a vertical, diagonal, or horizontal plane.

HANDLE GRIP. All throwing knives can be gripped and thrown by the handle. However, remember not to put the hilt or any part of the bolster on your palm. Otherwise, it could catch on the palm and will result in inconsistent and inaccurate throws.

Thick-handled knives such as the AK-47 bayonet or thin-handled knives such as the VM Bulalakaw can be thrown by the handle using the *curled finger handle grip*. In this grip, the thumb is placed on top of the handle with the tips of the other three big fingers on the opposite side. The edge of the knife can be oriented facing up, down (Figure 56), to the right (Figure 57), or to the left.

Thin- or thick-handled knives can also be thrown by the handle using the *wraparound grip*. Here, the fingers are wrapped around the handle with the thumb pressing on the index finger. Obviously, the wraparound grip cannot be used on knives with very short handles since part of the blade can become enclosed in the palm.

Held in the wraparound grip the knife can be thrown either with its point forward (*forward hold*) or with its point downward (*ice-pick hold*). The forward hold can be used on a thin-handled (Figure 53B) or on a thick-handled (Figure 58A) knife. The ice-pick hold (Figure 58B) can only be used with consistency and accuracy on thick-handled knives such as the K-Bar and the AK-47 bayonet.

BLADE VS. HANDLE GRIP. For the knife, gripping and throwing by the blade is as easy (or as difficult) as throwing by the handle. However, the latter is more practical.

Whether one grips and throws the knife by the handle or by the blade depends on the knife's design as well as on the time available for the throw. For example: Double-edged knives have to be gripped and thrown by the handle.

Army-type knives such as the K-Bar and the AK-47 bayonet have to be gripped and thrown by the handle for obvious reasons. Nobody fights hand-to-hand holding the knife by the blade. The need to throw the knife at any time, quickly, makes gripping and throwing army-type knives by the handle more practical. However, in a defensive situation and throwing from cover, there will be time to grip the knife by the blade.

THROWING A KNIFE

A knife can be thrown from above the left or right shoulder, from hip level at the left side or from beside the right leg.

FIGURE 54.

Curled finger blade grip on the VM Bulalakaw with its edge to the left.

FIGURE 55.

Straight finger blade grip on the VM Bulalakaw.

FIGURE 56.

Curled finger handle grip on the VM Bulalakaw with its edge down.

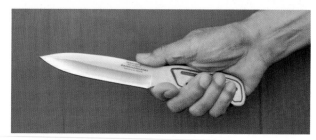

FIGURE 57.

Curled finger handle grip on the VM Bulalakaw with its edge to the right.

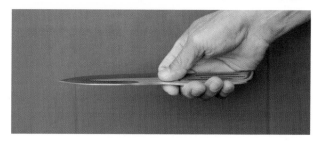

A knife can be given marked rotations about its longitudinal, medial, or transverse axes depending on the way it is gripped, the manner in which it is held, and the arm action. These are discussed in more detail in the section on spins and rotations.

Throwing a knife or any implement is basically safe—except for an occasional bad bounce, particularly when the target is wood. Using cardboard targets keeps you from having to duck a badly thrown knife.

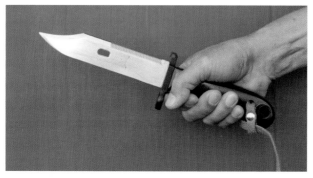

A. Forward hold

B. Ice-pick hold

FIGURE 58.

The wraparound grips on an AK-47 bayonet.

There is one other potential source of injury in the underhand throw. Once, using the forward hold on the AK-47 bayonet, I managed to put a hole in my pants and a cut on my leg. Though the wound was superficial, it was thoroughly annoying. To avoid making the same mistake again, I had to angle the bayonet slightly to the right. As soon as my arm passes my right leg, I turn my hand over slightly to point the knife at the target.

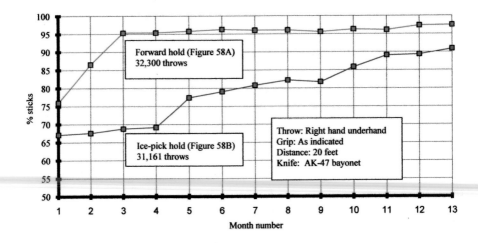

FIGURE 59.

My learning curves for my underhand throw using the forward and ice-pick holds on an AK-47 bayonet

---

LEARNING CURVE CASE STUDY

I became accurate with throwing the AK-47 bayonet using the forward hold rather quickly. Of course, all the other throws I made shortened my learning

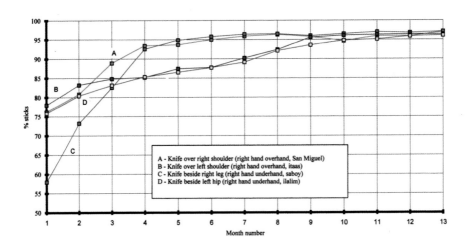

FIGURE 60.

My learning curves for my right-hand throws from four different throwing positions (Figures 7–10).

---

curve for this particular throw. It was not so for the underhand throw where I gripped the bayonet in the unusual ice-pick grip.

I had an accuracy of about 67 percent in my first month of throwing underhand using the ice-pick hold compared to about 77 percent for the overhand throw. Attesting to the difficulty of throwing the AK-47 bayonet underhand using the ice-pick grip is approximately 12 percent difference in sticking percentage in the thirteenth month.

THROWING WITH MY RIGHT HAND FROM FOUR DIFFERENT POSITIONS.
My sticking percentage, throwing with my right hand initially positioned over my left shoulder (B, Figure 8) and beside my left hip (D, Figure 10), are almost the same. But I got better quicker when I threw from my right side over my right shoulder (A, Figure 7) and from beside my right leg (C, Figure 9). Eventually after the ninth month, there is little difference between my sticking percentage from the four initial throwing positions.

After the thirteenth month, I felt I reached the limit of my throwing accuracy for these throws. At this point, I decided to learn other knife throws.

TRAJECTORY OF A THROWN KNIFE

Throw a knife some distance, observe its rotation, and compare it to that of a properly thrown football. The football will corkscrew, rotating smoothly around one axis, toward the receiver. On the other hand, a knife thrown into the air will rotate around three axes. Thus, the knife will seem to spin erratically.

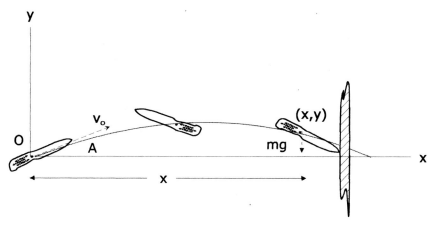

FIGURE 61.
The position of a knife in flight (not drawn to scale).

The motion of the knife is not erratic. It is simply rotating about its *center of mass* (CM), the point in the knife about which its mass (*m*) is evenly distributed. Mass is not easily understood, but weight is so I use the more common term *center of gravity* (CG). The CG can be located by balancing the knife over a pencil or over your finger.

The CG of the thrown knife will follow a curved path the shape of which is determined by gravity and by air resistance. The thrown knife will become a projectile, and its CG will trace a *parabolic* curve called its *trajectory*. The trajectory of a knife does not depend on its weight.

We can locate a knife at any point in its trajectory (Figure 61).

Here the knife is released at an angle (A) to the horizontal and with its CG at point O. After traveling a distance of x feet, it hits the target.

The coordinates, the position of the knife, at any time are shown as (x, y). The x-coordinate, in terms of the time of flight *t* is

$$x = (v_0 \cos A)t \qquad \text{(Equation 4)}$$

and the y-coordinate is

$$y = (v_0 \sin A)t - \frac{1}{2}gt^2. \qquad \text{(Equation 5)}$$

Solving for *t* in Equation 4 then substituting it into Equation 5 yields

$$y = x\tan A - \frac{g}{2v_o^2\cos^2 A}x^2 \qquad \text{(Equation 6)}$$

In the special case where y = 0 (Figure 62),

$$x = R = \frac{v_o^2}{g}\sin 2A \qquad \text{(Equation 7)}$$

The maximum height the knife can get to is

$$h = \frac{v_o^2\sin^2 A}{2g} \qquad \text{(Equation 8)}$$

The quantities x and R are related to the sticking distance (Equation 2, page 34 and Equation 3, page 36), that is,

Sticking distance =
x (or R) + horizontal distance from the CG to the tip of the knife

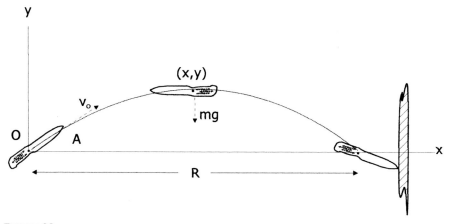

FIGURE 62.

The special case where y = 0, x = R, where R is the *range*. (Not drawn to scale.)

AX

SELECTING AN AX

There are a limited number of commercially available throwing axes (tomahawks). Should you want to start throwing an ax, buy the first one you see as most of them have wooden handles, are single-headed, and throw equally well. I own several commercial single-headed steel axes of identical design. I would not recommend this for beginning ax throwers.

DESIGNING MY AX

Most axes (tomahawks) that are commercially sold have wooden handles. A throwing ax (tomahawk) with a wooden handle will not last indefinitely. Eventually, the handle will become loose or will break, and this is very likely to happen early on when you are just starting to learn how to throw the ax (tomahawk).

I wanted an ax that I could throw as soon as I got it out of the box, without having to modify it. I also wanted an ax that could withstand frequent and prolonged use. This kind of ax is not commercially available, so I decided to design and fabricate my own, based on the following criteria:

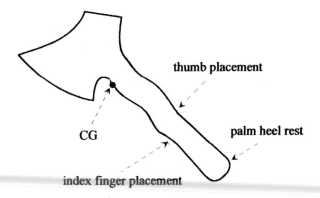

FIGURE 63.

The ax that I designed and fabricated, the VCM Palakol, has an undulating handle that ensures the proper placement of the thumb and the index finger for each throw. The shape of the upper edge and the sharp angle of its point maximize the possibility of the ax sticking to the target both in the underhand and overhand throws.

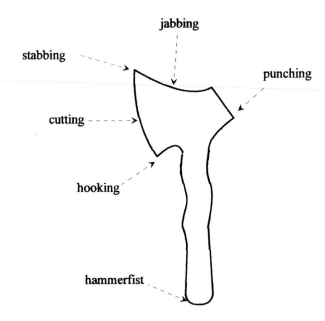

FIGURE 64.

For hand-to-hand combat, the VCM Palakol can be used for jabbing, cutting, or stabbing. It can also be used for puncturing or as a fist load for delivering a hammer-fist.

A.

B.

C.

FIGURE 65.

Hand-to-hand combat grips. The VCM Palakol can be gripped in three different ways for hand-to-hand combat. These grips can also be used for cutting wood.

1. Its handle must allow a comfortable grip when the ax is used as a cutting tool, a secure grip when used as a fighting tool, and a quick-release grip when used as a throwing tool.
2. It must be heavy enough to cut wood with ease, to ensure deep penetration when thrown, and to inflict deep puncture wounds in hand-to-hand combat.

I scoured the hardware stores in my neighborhood and found a 1' x 1' x ¼" steel plate that cost about $25. I traced my ax design on the ½-inch steel plate and was able to squeeze in three axes. There was even enough steel left for two knives.

It was not easy making the axes. I only had a hacksaw to cut them with and went through three cutting blades. Straight cuts were difficult enough; the curves took the most time and the most effort. I used a combination of a rough file, bench grinder, belt sander, and a Dremel attachment to rough-shape, smooth, and sharpen the axes. Two months later, I finished the axes and couldn't wait to throw them.

I had no problem throwing the ¼-inch thick ax underhand. However, it turned out to be too heavy for me in the overhand throw. For this reason, I looked for thinner steel plates, found ³⁄₁₆-inch thick steel plates at a welding shop, and fabricated a lighter ax using the same technique.

GRIPPING AN AX

There are a limited number of grips you can use on an ax. Unlike a knife, which can be thrown by the blade, you cannot grip an ax by its head for throwing. An ax can only be thrown by gripping its handle.

The curled finger handle grip used on the ax in the overhand throw is shown in Figure 66. Here, the thumb is held on top of the handle just before the hump. At the same time, the index finger is placed just before the hump under the handle. This prevents the thumb and the index finger from being placed too far forward. The bottom of the handle presses comfortably against the heel of the palm.

FIGURE 66.

The curled finger handle grip on the VCM Palakol (in the overhand throw) where the thumb is held about two inches from its CG.

A.

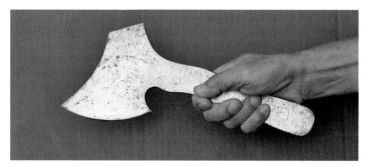

B.

FIGURE 67.

The curled finger handle grips on the VCM Palakol in the underhand throw.

The curled finger handle grip can be used on the ax in a unique way (Figure 67A) where the thumb and index finger are held at its CG. The index finger is placed close to the throat of the ax while the other three fingers are placed at the concave portion on the underside of the handle. The ax can also be held with the thumb and index finger a couple of inches away from the CG (Figure 67B).

THROWING AN AX

An ax may be thrown overhand or underhand. Thrown underhand, both the swing back and the swing forward must imitate the swing of a pendulum in one plane. Any deviation from a pendulum-like forward swing will result in an ax that will wobble toward the target.

A properly thrown ax will spin end over end and rotate only about its medial axis. An ax that wobbles could hit the target with its side and not with its point.

The ax impacts the target as it rotates downward. As a result, it pulls down the cardboard. For this reason, you might find it useful to nail the cardboard to the plywood backing at the top. (I drive in the nail just deep enough to pierce through the eight layers of cardboard and bite slightly into the plywood.) Expect to replace the first four layers of cardboard after about twenty throws because they become mutilated.

I did not make the point of my ax too sharp because I wanted the plywood backing to last as long as possible. Still, after 5,000 overhand throws, I had to turn the plywood so I could throw at a still hole-free part. By adjusting the placement of the plywood, I managed to make two panels last for 17,300 overhand throws.

It takes about twenty minutes to throw an ax one hundred times, sometimes longer.

LEARNING CURVE CASE STUDY

It will seem that I became very accurate throwing the ax very quickly. Not really. I still had to go through the frustration zone.

I started to throw the ax much later than the knife. However, there is no difference in the mechanics of throwing a knife and an ax. Hence, while I was throwing a knife, I was actually learning the mechanics of throwing an ax. Thus, my learning curve for the ax throw was shortened. This accounts for my high sticking average (Figure 68) right from the beginning.

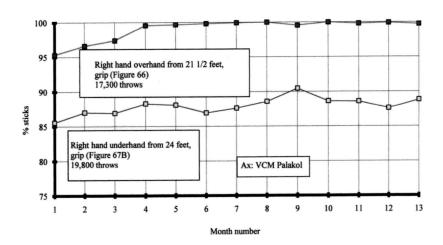

FIGURE 68.

My learning curves for my right-hand underhand and overhand throws using the same curled finger handle grip on the VCM Palakol.

My sticking average for the overhand ax throw is better than 99 percent. My sticking average for the underhand ax throw is about 10 percent lower. It is easier to make the ax rotate around its medial axis in the overhand throw than in the underhand throw. The ax tends to wobble more in the underhand throw.

The weight of a throwing knife or ax could affect your sticking average. For example: In the first three months, I used the heavy VCM Palakol. In month 3, I averaged about 97 percent. In the fourth month, I started using another VCM Palakol that was 25 percent lighter. With a lighter VCM Palakol, my average went up to better than 99 percent.

I missed sticking the heavier VCM Palakol 163 times out of 4,500 overhand throws. I missed sticking the lighter VCM Palakol 31 times out of 12,800 overhand throws.

SPEAR

SELECTING A SPEAR

A spear can be all steel with its point being an integral part of the shaft. This type of spear can be heavy; hence, it can be as short as 24 inches. However, a short spear will tend to rotate faster about its center of gravity than a longer spear and will require more skill to throw.

A spear can also be made completely from wood with its point hardened in a fire. A wooden spear will lose its sharpness when thrown repeatedly. However, it has the advantage of being light, so can be made longer, which will make it easier to throw. Also a wooden spear dulled by repeated throws or one that gets lost after a throw can be easily replaced.

The most common spear is one with a wooden shaft topped by a steel point (Figure 69). Such a spear combines the advantage of the light shaft and a steel point that will retain its sharpness even after repeated throws. But be aware that repeated throws will eventually loosen the connection where the metal and the wood are joined.

MAKING MY OWN SPEAR

The three sticks I use for stick fighting are the 31-inch *yantok*, the 36-inch *yantok*, and the 44-inch *pingga*, so I chose to make spears with shafts of these lengths (Figure 70). For the tips, I used discarded blades from the Philippine balisong. (Since I practice with the balisong, I usually have a few with broken handles, and so I have blades that can be readily made into spearpoints.)

The balisong's blade is connected to the spear handle with two pins (Figure 71). A third pin is used as a stop to keep the balisong rigid when opened. I had to grind this third pin until it was flush with the blade, and then using a nail, I hammered it out from its hole.

I used a saw to cut away a slit (about 2 inches deep) on the wooden shaft, then widened the slit with a knife to accommodate the thickness of the blade. I placed the blade on the side of the shaft, marked the holes, then drilled them.

I inserted the blade in the slit, inserted a nail through each hole, and cut the excess lengths of the nails with a hacksaw. To prevent the nails from dropping out, I wrapped duct tape around them. However, since each nail is slightly smaller than the diameter of the hole in the blade, there is some movement in the connection. But it is tolerable. Eventually, the nails will bend, then shear. When that happens, I can simply unwrap the duct tape and replace the nails.

The 44-inch spears I made cost me practically nothing since the wooden shafts I used were from pallets that were going to be thrown away. I made my 36-inch spears from 1" x 2" x 6' pine which costs under $3. Alternatively, you can use the much heavier 1" x 2" x 4' red oak which costs under $4 or the much lighter 1" x 2" x 4' poplar which costs under $3. A box of sixty 6D finish nails cost about $1. A 60-yard roll of duct tape costs under $5.

To reduce blade movement, I inserted the blade with only 2¼" of its length showing and drilled a

FIGURE 69.

Two spears with wooden shafts topped with balisong blades.

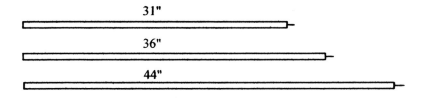

31"

36"

44"

FIGURE 70.

The three lengths of spear I throw: overhand (top and middle) and underhand (bottom). My targets consist of eight layers (about 1½" thick) of cardboard.

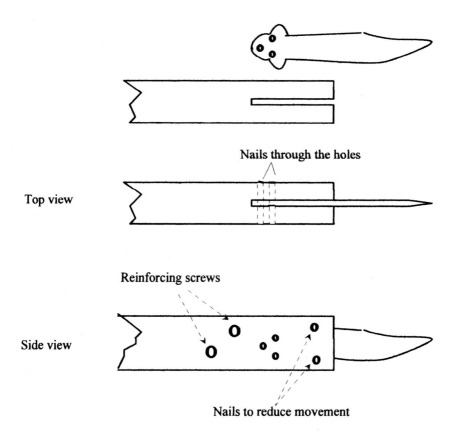

Top view

Nails through the holes

Side view

Reinforcing screws

Nails to reduce movement

FIGURE 71.

Details of my spear head. I reinforced the wood with two screws to prevent it from splitting. However, I found later that there was no need for this.

hole on each side, then inserted a nail in each hole. It is easier to make this kind of spear using wood with a rectangular cross section. The wood can be cut to the preferred length, trimmed, and the edges rounded to fit your grip.

GRIPPING A SPEAR

The grip on a spear will depend on the cross section of its shaft and on whether it is thrown overhand or underhand.

GRIP IN THE OVERHAND THROW. The spear can be gripped at its CG and with its shaft resting on the thumb (Figure 72A). This will tilt the shaft downward.

A.

B.

FIGURE 72.

Grips on a spear in the overhand throw. In A, the spear rests on the thumb. I prefer to wrap my fingers around its shaft (B).

As a result, the spear has to be thrown at a steeper angle. This grip is better used on spears with small cross sections.

Spears with larger cross sections have to be gripped with the fingers wrapped around its shaft (Figure 72B). This will allow throwing the spear at a shallower angle. I grip the shaft with the bottom of my fist at its CG.

GRIP IN THE UNDERHAND THROW. I grip a 44-inch spear about three inches behind its CG (Figure 75A) when I throw it underhand from 17–26 feet. (This is analogous to gripping a knife with its heavier end, either the blade or the

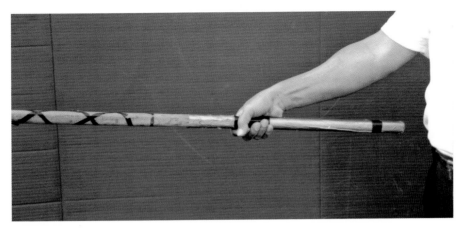

FIGURE 73.

The grip I use on a spear in the underhand throw.

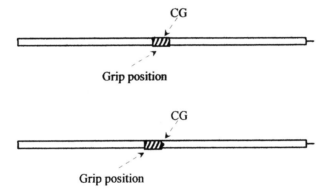

FIGURE 74.

Grip positions in the overhand throw. A spear can be gripped at its CG (top). However, I prefer to throw a spear with the bottom of my fist touching its CG (bottom).

handle, to the front.) Also try gripping the spear farther back to hit the target point first from a farther distance (Figure 75B).

THROWING A SPEAR

A throwing knife may be held so that at the time of release either its butt or its tip points in the direction of the target. On the other hand, if a spear is to hit point first, its tip must point toward the target at all times.

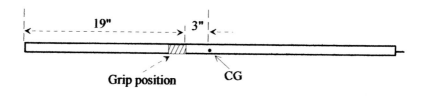

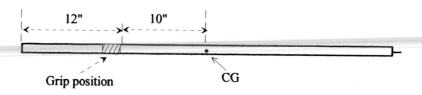

FIGURE 75.

Grip positions in the underhand throw. I hold a 44-inch spear 19 inches from its lower end when I throw it from 17–26 feet (top); from farther away, 12 inches from its lower end (bottom).

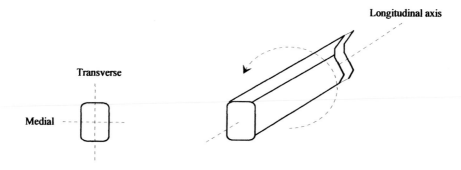

FIGURE 76.

Axes of rotation of a spear. To stabilize a spear in flight in the underhand throw, it must be made to rotate about its longitudinal axis. In the overhand throw, this rotation is not necessary.

This means that the flight of the spear must be controlled such that it will have little or no rotation about its transverse and medial axes. However, to stabilize the spear in its flight, it has to be made to rotate around its longitudinal axis (Figure 76). This is achieved by making the spear roll inside the palm as the throw progresses.

The spear must be thrown in such a manner so as to prevent it from stalling or spinning. If the angle of attack (Figure 77A) is too steep or if it is held at the wrong location (Figure 77B), the tip of the spear will tend to rise causing it to stall.

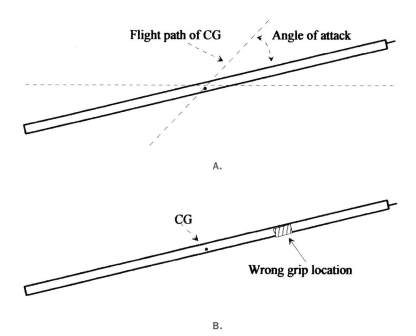

Flight path of CG   **Angle of attack**

A.

CG

Wrong grip location

B.

FIGURE 77.

The tip of a spear will tend to rise if the angle of attack is too steep (A) or if it is gripped in the wrong location (B).

FIGURE 78.

In the underhand throw, the wrist must be bent such that the spear leaves the hand parallel to the ground.

FIGURE 79.

Grip change on the shaft in the overhand throw. The initial closed grip (Figure 72B) changes to the open grip at the time of release.

UNDERHAND THROW. Throw a spear underhand such that at the time of release (a) its shaft is aligned with the ground, (b) its shaft does not come in contact with your forearm, and (c) your fingers are pointing at the target. Like the throwing of a knife, there is the required smooth follow-through.

Wrist action (Figure 78) in the underhand throw is very important. In the beginning of the throw, the wrist must be relaxed. As the throw progresses, it

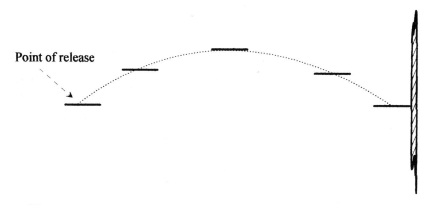

Point of release

FIGURE 80.

At close distances, a spear can be thrown so that it leaves the hand parallel to the ground (top). From farther away, it has to be released at a steeper angle (bottom). Otherwise, it will dip too fast.

THE ART OF THROWING

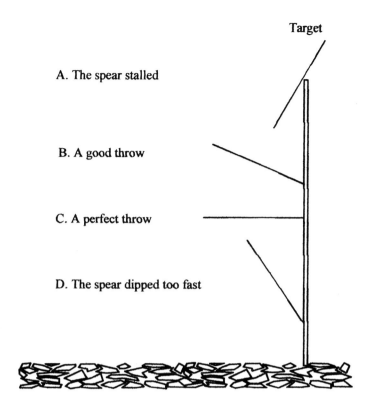

A. The spear stalled

B. A good throw

C. A perfect throw

D. The spear dipped too fast

Target

FIGURE 81.

Possible angles of impact of a thrown spear.

bends more. At the time of release, the wrist is bent to the maximum—close to becoming uncomfortable.

OVERHAND THROW. In the overhand throw, at the time of release (a) a spear's shaft must be angled above the horizontal, (b) the fingers must be pointing at the target and (c) the spear must be perpendicular to the face of the target. At the time of release any slight motion to the right or left will cause the spear to drift to the side. In the required smooth follow-through, the open palm ends between the level of the shoulder and the hip.

Grip the spear, initially, with your fingers wrapped around its shaft and with the bottom of your fist at its CG. As the forward swing of your arm progresses, straighten your fingers (Figure 79) to allow the smooth release of the spear. To increase the power in the throw, lean your body forward but not to the point of imbalance.

I wanted to compare my underhand and overhand throws, so I generated this learning curve.

From the defensive standpoint (if you happen to have a spear at hand when there is a need for it), it is better to throw a spear underhand for the following reasons:

1. The underhand throw omits the act of raising the spear which will save precious time.
2. The underhand throw is more likely to come as a surprise because the spear is held at the lower side and seems to pose no threat. On the other hand, the initial position of the spear in the overhand throw is very aggressive and threatening.
3. The spear is normally heavy.

UNDERHAND VS. OVERHAND THROW. In the first month, my sticking percentage for the overhand throw was lower than for the underhand throw. However, in the subsequent months, I hardly missed sticking the spear in the overhand throw.

UNDERHAND THROW. The mechanics of the underhand throw are the same for any throwing implement. The timing of the release, the swing of the arm, and

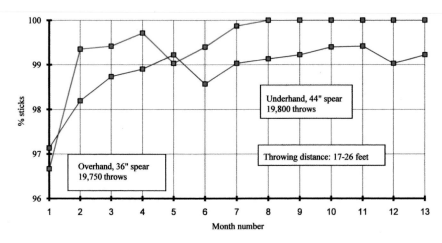

FIGURE 82.

My sticking percentage for the right-hand overhand and underhand spear throws.

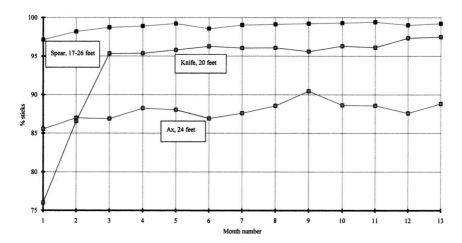

FIGURE 83.

A comparison of my sticking percentages for the right-hand underhand throws for the spear, ax, and knife.

---

the smooth follow-through were merely carried over to my spear throws. Hence, the curve shows no frustration zone. (I learned to throw the bagakay, knife, ax, and spear in that order, so the frustration zone for my bagakay throws can be considered also as the frustration zone for my ax and spear throws.)

The spear is the easiest implement to stick on the target because it is easier to suppress its rotation (about its medial and transverse axes). Besides, the spear is initially held then thrown with its tip pointed at the target. On the other hand, the knife and the ax spin end over end on the way to the target making throwing distance critical. In the spear throw, as long as you are able to get the spear to the target, there is a good chance that you can make it stick.

The knife has a more complex rotation than the ax. However, I have a better sticking average throwing the knife underhand. While the pendulum-like motion in the ax throw is the same as that in the spear throw, it is not easy to control the wobble of the ax because of its shape. Hence, I have a better sticking average with the knife.

The grips I used on the knife, ax, and spear are variations of the curled finger handle grips. In the ax and spear throws, my grip is behind the CG. On the knife, I place my thumb directly over its CG.

The throwing distance for the spear is *any* distance from which you can get the spear to the target. With the ax and the knife, it cannot be any distance: it must be such that it will allow both to make full spins.

- CHAPTER 3 -

JAPANESE THROWING IMPLEMENTS

While reading on the throwing of the Japanese shaken and shuriken, I came to recognize a major difference between the grips they use and the grips I use: the shuriken is gripped at the center of gravity.

I have thrown shuriken-like implements (such as the bagakay, ice picks, and chopsticks) before. However, I have gripped the throwing implement with its center of gravity just beyond my index finger's tip or about an inch away from it—not in my grasp. I decided to experiment with the Japanese method of gripping the shuriken.

The shuriken can be thrown in three ways: with no, half, or full spins. The no spin throw is particularly effective from as far as 18 feet. However, from longer distances, it becomes very difficult to get the shuriken to hit the target point first using this technique.

The one-pointed shuriken, when held with its point forward, will stick when it makes full spins; with its point toward the back, when it makes half spins. However, held one way or the other, the shuriken has to be thrown from a set distance.

The problem of distance is somewhat reduced when throwing a two-pointed shuriken, which obviously will stick whether it reaches the target on half or full spins. However, it still has to be thrown from a specific distance. This problem is magnified when the target is an enemy in motion.

An obvious solution to the problem of distance is the use of a many-pointed implement such as the shaken. The shaken will stick whether it makes full spins or fractions of a spin—from *any* distance.

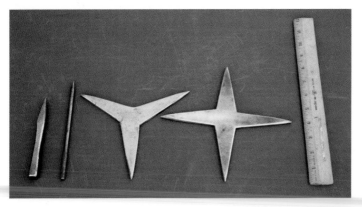

A.

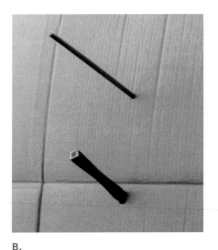

B.

D.

C.

FIGURE 84.

Japanese throwing implements (A) left to right: negishi-ryu shuriken, shirai-ryu shuriken, three-pointed shaken, and four-pointed shaken. Shown embedded on my cardboard targets are shirai-ryu and negishi-ryu shurikens (B), a three-pointed shaken (C), and a four-pointed shaken (D).

SHURIKEN

The Japanese shuriken has its counterpart in the Philippine bagakay and Chinese flying sticker. The shuriken can be one- or two-pointed with lengths ranging from five to ten inches.

The shuriken can be flat, round, octagonal or with nonuniform cross sections. The shape of the shuriken identifies the particular Japanese martial arts school (Figure 84) that uses it.

The shuriken is relatively light; two or three can be carried without causing any discomfort. This will allow subsequent throws if the first throw misses or if faced by more than one opponent.

MAKING MY OWN SHURIKEN

The negishi-ryu shuriken and the shirai-ryu shuriken are not difficult to make.

NEGISHI-RYU SHURIKEN. The negishi-ryu shuriken is not readily available in the United States. Fortunately, photographs and diagrams of negishi-ryu shurikens are illustrated in the book *Shuriken-Do* by the Japanese master Shirakami Ikku-ken.

I made wooden models of the negishi-ryu shurikens based on (a) the relative dimensions of the tapers and the flares, and (b) the length of the point that protrudes past the middle finger. Hence, built into the models are the lengths of my thumb and middle finger. After numerous filings and subsequent fittings, I felt confident that I could make a shuriken without ruining the first steel bar I would work on.

The negishi-ryu shuriken is held over the middle finger. It is squeezed by the index and ring fingers and pressed down with the thumb held nearly at right angles to the shuriken. I placed the bent thumb on the narrow waist. The negishi-ryu type shurikens I made are $5\frac{5}{8}$ inches, 6 inches, and 8 inches long. Its point juts $\frac{1}{2}$-inch past the tip of my middle finger.

I made negishi-ryu type shurikens (Figure 85) from square steel bars. I had the steel bars cut to the proper length, rough-shaped the bars into shurikens with hexagonal cross sections using a file and a bench grinder, then smoothed them using a file and a belt sander.

SHIRAI-RYU SHURIKEN. The shurikens of the shirai-ryu school have circular cross sections and are easier to make. Steel rods with lengths of thirty-six inches and with different diameters are readily available in hardware stores or in welding shops. A $\frac{1}{4}$-inch diameter 36-inch steel rod, in a hardware store, costs about

$4. In a welding shop, it costs less than half that. Even better is that the welding shop will cut the rod to the length you specify.

I tapered one end to a sharp point using a bench grinder (Figure 85).

Gripping a shuriken

A shuriken can be gripped with its sharp point up. It is held with a slight slant to the right with its length on the middle finger and is squeezed on each side by the index and ring fingers. At the same time, the thumb is placed on top to secure the grip.

It can also be gripped with its point on the palm. This kind of grip will not present any problem if you throw only occasionally. However, if you throw shurikens, say, one hundred times in one practice session, the repeated contact of the point on the palm can be annoying.

The shuriken can also be gripped like a knife or two-pointed bagakay. In these grips, either the dull end rests on the palm but not at its center or the sharp point is in the palm but its tip hardly touches the skin.

The two grips on the shuriken (that are consistent with those I use on throwing knives) are:

1. handle grip where the shuriken is held with its point away from the thrower
2. blade grip where the shuriken is held with its point toward the thrower

The characteristics of the handle (Figure 86) will determine the speed of the release. For example, a shuriken with a tapered handle (Figure 86, left) should release quickly. If the grip is not tight enough, the thrown shuriken will fall short of the target. To avoid premature release, it should be gripped more tightly. A higher arc will compensate for a quick release. However, a higher arc could result in inaccurate throws.

If the shuriken tapers then flares (Figure 86, right), this will allow it to stay longer in the hand, thus allowing better control of the release. While the difference in release times is mere split seconds, this is the difference between a good and a bad throw.

The narrow waist of the shuriken ensures a consistent placement of the thumb from one throw to the next. Both the thumb and middle finger are placed on flared portions of the waist and of the point. If there is no flare, the thrower will need to squeeze harder on the shuriken to avoid a premature release.

A narrow waist is not unique to the shuriken but is also common in Swiss, German, and Spanish throwing knives (Figure 87). You can find this characteristic narrow waist on many American throwing knives as well.

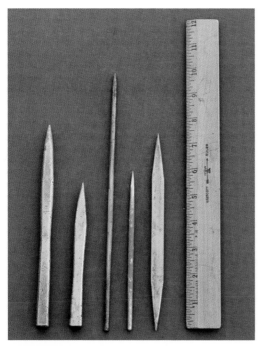

FIGURE 85.

Typical shapes of a shuriken: negishi-ryu (left two), shirai-ryu (middle two), and Shirakami Ikku-ken's (right).

FIGURE 86.

The shape of a shuriken will determine the speed of its release.

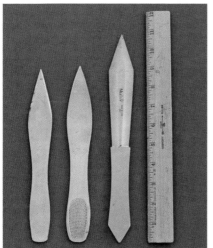

FIGURE 87.

Swiss, German, and Spanish throwing knives with characteristic narrow waists.

A.

Negishi-ryu grip. The dull end of the shuriken is placed at the center of the palm with the thumb pressing on its top and almost perpendicular to it.

B.

Jikishin grip. The dull end is in the palm with the index finger held along its length. This is almost like pointing a finger and a very natural grip.

C.

Shirai-ryu grip. The sharp tip of the shuriken is in the palm.

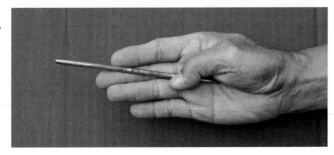

FIGURE 88.

Grips on the shuriken used by Japanese masters.

JAPANESE MASTERS' GRIPS. There is a great difference between the grips used by American knife throwers (myself included) and those used by the Japanese master Shirakami Ikku-ken, shirai-ryu, and negishi-ryu. This will seem to be superficial. But it is not. It is more basic than that.

In these grips, the shuriken is held such that its CG is in the palm. American knife throwers grip the knife with the heavier end to the front. This places the CG of the knife at, close to, or an inch or two past the index finger.

Ikku-ken places the shuriken on top of his middle finger. This grip is very comfortable for shurikens with cross sections that approximate the size of the middle finger (Figure 88A). The shirai-ryu school uses this grip on a shuriken

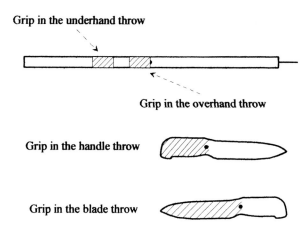

Grip in the underhand throw

Grip in the overhand throw

Grip in the handle throw

Grip in the blade throw

FIGURE 89.

The rule of thumb in throwing an implement is to have the heavier end to the front. The cross-hatch is the hand grip on the implement.

that has a small cross section (Figure 88C). One of the grips (Figure 88B) used by Shirakami Ikku-ken is quite unique. It is like pointing a finger at the target.

My grips. The general rule of thumb on gripping a knife or any throwing implement is to have the heavier end to the front (Figure 89).

I follow this rule when I throw a 7-inch shuriken (Figure 90A–B). This shuriken is light and the only way I feel comfortable throwing it is to hold it such that its dull tip rests on the edge of my ring finger (close to the little finger). Thus, its CG is about half an inch past the tip of my thumb. This gives me the feeling that I am throwing something.

The handle grips I use on a shuriken (Figure 91B, D) with the CG at, close to, or an inch or two past the tip of my thumb or index finger will make it an effective weapon in close-quarter fighting.

A.

B.

FIGURE 90.

I throw a 7" shirai-ryu shuriken with its CG about half an inch past the tip of my thumb.

A. This is similar to the straight finger blade grip I use on the bagakay. However, Japanese masters keep their thumbs almost perpendicular to the shuriken. My thumb is more on a diagonal.

B. The dull end is in the palm with the thumb held on top of the shuriken. This is the curled finger handle grip that I also use on the knife. This same grip can be used for close-quarter fighting. (See Figure 90A.)

C. The sharp tip is in the palm but barely touches it. This is the same curled finger blade grip I use on the knife. (See Figure 90B.)

D. The dull end of the 8" negishi-ryu shuriken is in the palm. This is the curled finger handle grip I also use on the knife.

FIGURE 91.

The grips I use on the shuriken.

THROWING A SHURIKEN

A light 6-inch shuriken should be thrown overhand. A longer and heavier shuriken can be thrown underhand without any problem.

The shuriken will spin counterclockwise (viewed from the right side of the thrower) about its CG when thrown overhand. This spin is imparted to the shuriken by the rotation of the throwing arm about the shoulder.

A shuriken may be thrown with no spin, half spins, or full spins.

NO SPIN. In the no spin throw, a shuriken is gripped with its point toward the target in much the same way as when a spear is thrown. For the no spin throw, horsehair is attached to the tail of the shuriken. Even with such artifice, the thrower still has to apply moderate pressure with the index finger on the tail at the time of release to suppress its spin.

I throw the negishi-ryu shuriken at an angle of launch such that it will stall and just start to dip close to the target. This is accomplished by an abrupt downward movement of the throwing arm at the time of release. The index finger will prevent the shuriken from rotating. *This no spin throw can only be effected if the shuriken is released with the hand on a vertical.*

The no spin adds two more variables to a throw: the horsehair and the need to suppress the shuriken's spin; therefore it is more difficult than either the half or full spin throw.

HALF SPIN. In the half spin throw, the shuriken is gripped with its point toward the thrower (in much the same way that a knife is thrown by the blade). This is an easier throw than the no spin throw.

FULL SPIN. In the full spin throw, the shuriken is gripped with its point toward the target (in much the same way that a knife is thrown by the handle). This is the more practical throw for the shuriken, if it is to double as a weapon for

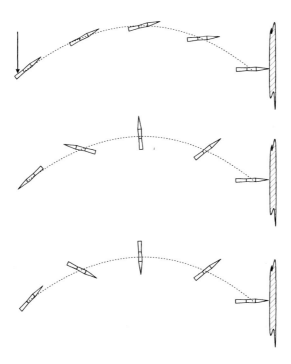

FIGURE 92.

The trajectory of a one-pointed shuriken making no spin (top), half spin (middle), and one full spin (bottom). The downward arrow (top) indicates pressure applied with the index finger on the shuriken to suppress its spin.

close-quarter fighting. In books on the shuriken written by Japanese authors, its use in close-quarter fighting has been mentioned.

The shuriken is easier to throw if you allow it to spin end over end. However, like the throwing of any implement (except for the shaken or the spear), to make it stick, it has to be thrown from a given distance.

THROWING DISTANCE

I do not have firsthand contact with the negishi-ryu school. However, Shirakami Ikku-ken has summarized the negishi-ryu shuriken and their throwing methods. Essentially,

1. The negishi-ryu throws the shuriken using the "direct" hit method. Direct hit means no spin. The maximum throwing distance according to the Japanese master is 18.1 feet.
2. The negishi-ryu uses shurikens that have tassels made from threads and from bear or horsehair, which according to their lengths are made for throwing from a short, middle, or long distances. The length of the tassel determines the location of the center of gravity of the shuriken. The school uses shurikens with no tails for throwing from a short distance.
3. The negishi-ryu trains to throw from a long distance a shuriken designed for throwing from a short distance.

The throwing distance will depend on (a) the grip used on the implement, (b) the location of its CG, and to a lesser extent (c) length of the implement. The effect of the grip used on the throwing (sticking) distance is illustrated in Table 7.

TABLE 7. Grips and throwing distances using one- and two-pointed 8" negishi-ryu type shuriken.

Number of spins	Grip		Distance*, feet
	one-pointed	*two-pointed*	
0	handle	handle or blade	
½	blade	handle or blade	9
1	handle	handle or blade	21
1½	blade	handle or blade	28
2	handle	handle or blade	40

* See Chapter 1, "Throwing and sticking distances."

What grip would you use to throw from 15', 25', 35', and other "in-between" distances?

The in-between distances can be bridged with a shift of the location of the CG, not within the shuriken (effected by varying the length of the tassel) but by gripping it farther up or down the handle. Therefore a longer negishi-ryu shuriken makes more sense, otherwise, you could run out of shuriken to hold. For this reason, I used an 8-inch shuriken to generate Table 7.

It is obvious that it is more efficient to throw a two-pointed shuriken than one with only one point, since you do not need to switch from the handle to the blade grip. Or better yet, throw the many-pointed shaken instead.

LEARNING CURVE CASE STUDY

NO SPIN VS. WITH SPIN THROW. From Figure 96, it is apparent that the no spin throw becomes less accurate when the distance is greater than eighteen feet. Hence, at longer distances, the half spin or full spin throws are more practical.

In Figure 97, I compared my sticking percentage for the no spin and the two full spins throw. However, I used a longer shuriken in the full spins throw and a shorter shuriken in the no spin throw.

Throwing an 8-inch shuriken from twenty-two feet with no spin, I tried hard to suppress its spin, but I couldn't. This is understandable, because the CG of

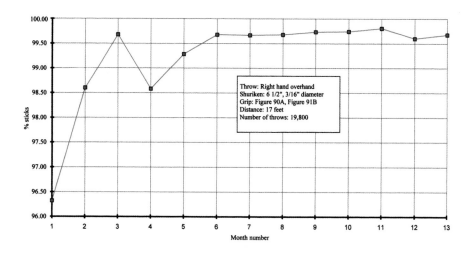

FIGURE 93.

My learning curve throwing a shirai-ryu type shuriken using the curled finger handle grip (Figures 90A, 91B).

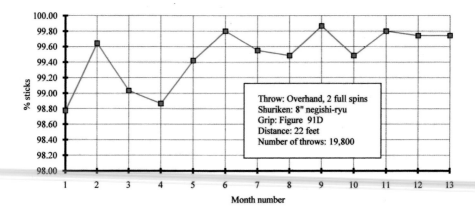

FIGURE 94.

My sticking average throwing a 8" negishi-ryu type shuriken from 22 feet gripping it in the same way as when I throw a knife by the handle.

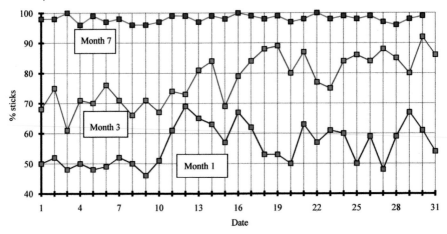

FIGURE 95.

My sticking percentage for three non-consecutive months throwing a 5⅝" negishi-ryu type shuriken with no spin from 18 feet using the negishi-ryu grip (Figure 88A).

the longer shuriken is more to the front than that of the shorter shuriken. I also tried throwing a 5⅝-inch shuriken, with two full spins, from twenty-one feet. However, the 8-inch shuriken is more accurate from longer distances than the shorter shuriken.

Shirakami Ikku-ken does not mention throwing the negishi-ryu shuriken other than in the no spin throw. However, I found that the 8-inch and the 5⅝-inch shurikens work well with the underhand throw.

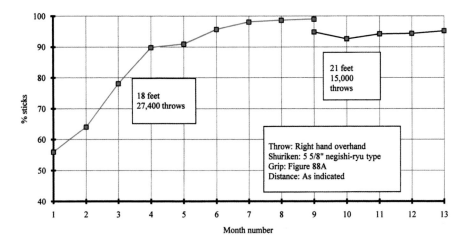

FIGURE 96.

My learning curve for the no spin throw for a negishi-ryu type shuriken using the negishi-ryu grip. There is a big difference in my averages throwing the 5⅝" shuriken from 18 feet and from 21 feet.

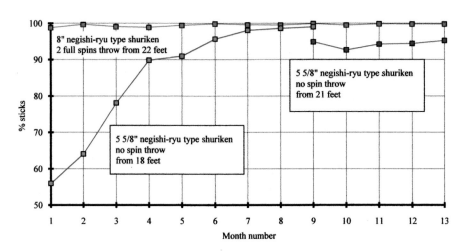

FIGURE 97.

A comparison of my sticking averages throwing a 5⅝" shuriken using the no spin throw and the full spins throw.

Figure 97 shows my averages for the no spin and the two full spins throw. The graph indicates that at longer distances, it is more practical, indeed necessary, to throw a shuriken with a spin.

JIKISHIN GRIP. The jikishin grip (Figure 88B) is the name used by Shirakami Ikku-ken for when the shuriken is held with its dull end on the palm and with the index finger placed along its length. Ikku-ken does not mention the distance from which he used this grip. Nor does he mention if he threw it with a spin.

I thought that, since its CG is on my palm, I would be able to throw the shuriken with no spin in much the same way when I used the negishi-ryu grip. However, I was not able to suppress its spin.

After several throws, I determined that the first throwing distance, using this grip on a 5⅝-inch negishi-ryu shuriken is about 24 feet. From this distance, it takes a full spin before it will stick on the target. The next throwing distance is about 52 feet, which is not practical for a defensive throw—unless you are throwing from ambush.

Note that in the jikishin grip, the shuriken starts to spin after it has passed the midpoint of the throw.

SHAKEN

A knife thrown in the blade grip will stick on a target if it completes ½, 1½, 2½ spins and so on. A knife (or ax) thrown in the handle grip will stick when it completes 1, 2, 3 spins and so on. See Figure 17. This means that for a knife to stick on the target, it must be thrown from a certain distance.

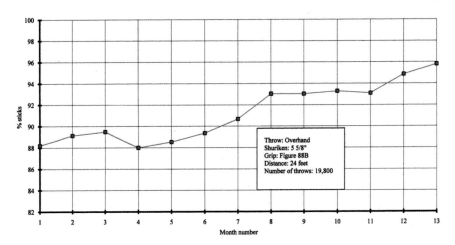

FIGURE 98.

My learning curve using the jikishin grip on a negishi-ryu type shuriken.

Spinning is not the desired behavior if a spear is to stick to the target. It has to be held and thrown with its tip pointing in the direction of the target at all times.

Unlike a knife or an ax, a bagakay, because it is two-pointed, will stick on the target when it completes ½, 1, 1½, 2, 2½, 3, ... spins. It is obvious then that (if the distance to the target is not known) there is a greater possibility of a two-pointed throwing implement sticking on a target than a one-pointed one.

It follows that if a throwing implement is many-pointed, it will be easier to make it stick on the target. The implement will stick after any number of full spins or fractions of spins. It does not matter what the distance is from where it is thrown. Such an implement will be an ideal defensive throwing weapon because distances are never constant in a conflict. Two such throwing implements are the Chinese throwing star and the Japanese shaken.

A shaken can have three, four, five, six, or as many as eight projecting points (Figure 99). One will rarely miss sticking it. The only disadvantage of the shaken is that it is not convenient to carry. If accessed improperly, the carrier could get pricked or even stabbed by its many sharp points.

Shakens sold commercially are usually small and lighter than a throwing knife. However, what they lack in mass, they make up for in the number that can be carried on one's person and the rapid succession with which they can be thrown.

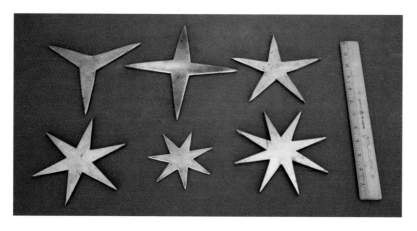

FIGURE 99.

Many-pointed shakens are easy enough to make. Since I used a hacksaw, I cut the steel at the rate of 7" a day. The maximum depth of penetration decreases as the number of projecting points increases because adjacent projecting points on each side of the one that sticks could get in the way (Figure 104, bottom).

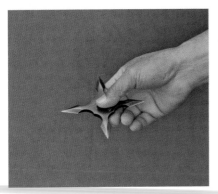

FIGURE 100.

The most common grip used on small sharp-edged shakens. The thumb and index finger are placed on opposite sides of the hole.

FIGURE 101.

The grip used by the Japanese master Shirakami Ikku-ken on oversized, dull-edged shakens. The last three fingers grip one of the projecting points. The thumb and index finger are held straight on opposite sides.

A.

B.

FIGURE 102.

Knife-like grips on many-pointed, dull-edged, oversized shakens. The shaken is gripped at one of its projecting points with the four fingers and the thumb.

MAKING MY OWN SHAKENS

I fabricate my own shakens because the shakens available in the market only partially satisfy the characteristics that I am looking for. I make my shakens with dull edges that allow more gripping options. For example, you cannot use the grips shown in Figures 103 and 106 on shakens with sharp edges.

I started with 3/16-inch thick rectangular steel plates that measured 12" x 6½", which were cut for me by the welding shop where I bought them. I made wooden models of the shakens. After I fitted and felt comfortable with the wooden model, I traced it on the steel plate.

Shakens can have holes in the middle through which a cord can be run for ease of carrying. A piece of wood can be inserted in the hole to make it easier to pull out deeply embedded shakens. The hole also allows a more secure grip.

While throwing regular-size shakens, I wondered how it would feel to throw bigger ones, so I made a few that are oversized. The 8⅛-inch four-pointed shakens I made dwarf those that are sold in martial arts stores. Because the

A.

B.

C.

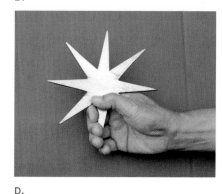

D.

FIGURE 103.

The overhand (A–D) and underhand (E) grips I use on oversized, dull-edged shakens.

E.

oversized shaken is big, it is also heavy. Thus, it can be thrown underhand and will stick with authority. It packs quite a wallop.

GRIPPING A SHAKEN

A shaken can be gripped in a number of ways for throwing (Figures 100–103): The grips illustrated will give you good control over the shaken. Your choice of grip will depend on the size of the shaken, the number of projecting points, and whether it has dull or sharp edges.

In the overhand throw, a shaken is supported on the "V" of the hand with the index finger and thumb touching (Figure 103A–D). The middle three fingers are placed on top of one projecting point. The little finger barely touches the shaken at the back. This allows a more secure grip for use of the shaken in close-quarter fighting and better control for throwing.

In the underhand throw, the shaken rests on the index, middle, and ring fingers (Figure 103E).

THROWING A SHAKEN

A shaken can be thrown overhand or underhand from the left or from the right using the grip of your choice. Since a shaken will stick from whatever distance it is thrown, the thrower can concentrate on hitting a small area of the target and need not be concerned with whether it will stick or not.

The mechanics of a shaken throw are the same as those for a knife, ax, or spear. The feet must be spaced apart and the knees bent comfortably. For the shaken to stick with authority:

1. the knees must unbend slightly in the underhand throw and bend slightly in the overhand throw
2. the hips must twist to reinforce the subsequent elbow action
3. the release and follow-through must be smooth
4. balance must be maintained at all times.

The throwing action must be such that at the time of release, the wrist is kept in one plane. Any inward or outward bending of the wrist will make the shaken wobble in its flight.

The shaken can be thrown horizontally, vertically, or diagonally.

The target must be small enough for you to develop accuracy in placing the shaken but still big enough to minimize the possibility of an incoming shaken

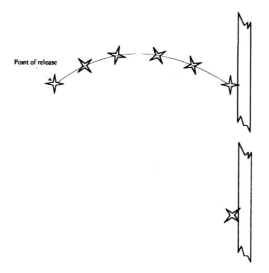

FIGURE 104.

Trajectory of a shaken. The shaken will stick whether it hits the target in fractions of a spin or in full spins.

hitting an already-embedded one. You can use the multiple targets shown in Figure 42. Sometimes I use rectangular 10" x 12" targets for the smaller three- and four-pointed shakens, and 12" x 14" targets for the bigger shakens. Mark the dimensions on the cardboard; then connect the dots. To further develop accuracy, use concentric rectangles.

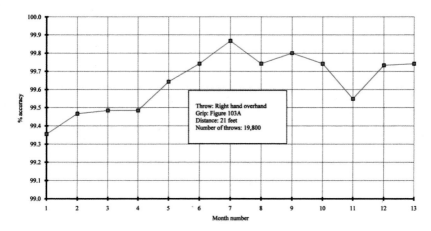

FIGURE 105.

My accuracy percentage throwing a four-pointed (5" across) shaken. The target is a 10" x 12" rectangle.

The shaken could hit with two of its points simultaneously sticking on the target (Figure 104, bottom). This requires replacing the cardboard target more often than when you throw one- or two-pointed implements.

OVERHAND THROW USING IKKU-KEN'S GRIP. The jikishin grip (Figure 88B) used by the Japanese master Ikku-ken on the one-pointed shuriken and the grip (Figure 101) he used on the four-pointed shaken are identical.

I was skeptical when I first saw the jikishin grip for the one-pointed shuriken. However, after having used the grip, I came to appreciate its merits. I thought it would be interesting to throw a three-pointed shaken using the same grip (Figure 106).

Then I came to appreciate its merits even more.

You will be less accurate with the three-pointed shaken than with the four-pointed shaken for two reasons. First, the same-size three-pointed shaken is at least 25 percent lighter than a four-pointed shaken. Second, the three-pointed shaken could hit "flat" as shown in Figure 107.

The lighter three-pointed shaken will pop out (more often than the four-pointed shaken) of the cardboard target even after hitting with its point.

COMMERCIAL 4-INCH SHAKEN THROWN FROM BESIDE THE LEFT HIP. Shakens sold commercially have needle-sharp points and razor-sharp edges. When you practice throwing them, you must exercise caution.

The most common way of throwing sharp-edged shakens is from beside the left hip. I have

FIGURE 106.

The grip I used on a three-pointed shaken.

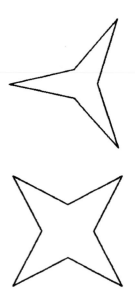

FIGURE 107.

The adjacent projecting points of a three-pointed shaken are farther apart than those of a four-pointed shaken.

thrown knives the same way. However, knives are easier to throw because they are much heavier.

Because shakens are light, they must be thrown energetically. The power in the throw is derived from the twisting of the hips, the straightening of the arm, and the unbending of the wrist.

If you have not thrown a shaken from this position before, expect to hurt the next day. The pain in the upper arm, sometimes in the shoulder joint, is tolerable but annoying. However, after a couple of days, it will go away.

In my first fifty throws, the shakens drifted to my right. To compensate for the drift, I moved about a foot to my left. In this throwing position my front toe was pointed toward the target. However, I prefer to throw the shaken with my right side at a right angle with the target. This throwing position minimizes the drift to the right.

- CHAPTER 4 -

～◆～

CHINESE THROWING IMPLEMENTS

The Chinese martial arts are well known for empty hand fighting systems as well as for weapons fighting systems. A wide variety of weapons, including swords, spears, knives, and staffs of varying sizes and shapes are part of the Chinese weapons fighting tradition.

While many Chinese weapons and empty hand fighting systems have become household words, there is a little known branch of study called hidden weapons.

These weapons are "hidden" in the sense that they are carried covertly on one's person and become visible only at the time of use or they are visible but are not designed for use as weapons or are so commonplace that most people will not consider them weapons (ordinary pebbles, for example).

This branch includes an extensive array of weapons, which can be grouped under three categories:

1. Weapons used to launch projectiles. These include the cylindrical dart, slingshot, bow and arrow, blowgun, and crossbow.
2. Weapons that are thrown but are tethered to a rope for quick recovery. These include the flying cymbal, mace, flying claw, rope dart, shooting star hammer, dragon's beard hook, whip-chain dart, and iron lotus.
3. Weapons that are thrown free of tethers from the hand. These include the flying dart, golden coin dart, flying steel olive, and flying sticker.

We will focus on the hidden weapons that are thrown freely. Of these hidden weapons, we will look at the flying dart, because of its unique shape and the

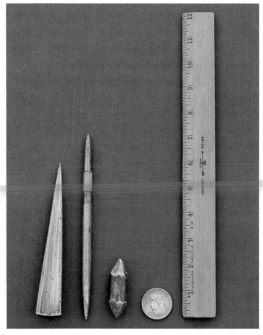

A.   B.

FIGURE 108.

Chinese throwing implements: (A, left to right) flying dart, flying sticker, flying olive, and golden coin dart. With practice, the flying dart and flying sticker can be made to stick on cardboard targets (B). However, it would take some sort of Herculean effort to get a golden coin dart or steel olive to stick on a cardboard target. The ideal target for the olive and the coin is a mound of earth or clay.

unique method with which it has to be thrown; the steel olive and golden coin dart, because of their unique shape and size: and the flying sticker, because of the unique grip with which it is thrown.

FLYING DART

The flying dart has a most unique shape. It has a "Y" cross section that tapers to a point. Two-inch long red and green silk tassels can be attached to a flying dart, which help suppress its natural tendency to spin.

The flying dart is usually less than 4 inches long and weighs about 6 ounces. Because it is relatively short and light, Chinese masters in the past carried a set of twelve or nine darts. In each set there is one flying dart that is longer and heavier than the rest that is used to deliver the *coup de grâce*.

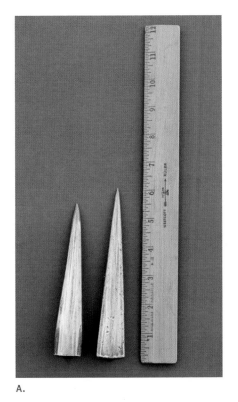

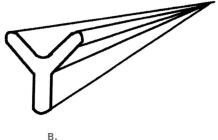

A.   B.

FIGURE 109.

Flying darts I fabricated from solid steel bars (A). The three grooves (B) make the dart unique.

MAKING MY OWN FLYING DARTS

It is difficult to find flying darts in the United States. I have a feeling that even in China, they may be difficult to find. So, you will most likely need to make your own.

I first made a 5-inch long wooden model. The making of the wooden model helped me plan how to execute the minimum number of cuts since I planned to construct my dart from a solid steel bar. I hacksawed, filed, ground, and smoothed the 1" x 1" cross section steel bar until, finally, I was able to finish one flying dart after a month.

FIGURE 110.

One of the grips that can be used on the flying dart where the thumb presses on one of the vanes.

A.

B.

FIGURE 111.

The grip I use on the flying dart. The middle finger is placed over the top groove. The dart is squeezed in place with the thumb on the left groove. The ring and index fingers (held straight) press at opposite sides at the top. The tail end is placed in the middle of the palm.

GRIPPING A FLYING DART

A flying dart can be gripped so that the middle finger is placed over the top groove and the thumb held perpendicular to the back fin (Figure 110). The ring and index fingers press on opposite sides of the dart at the top. This is similar to the grip used on a negishi-ryu shuriken where the shuriken is placed over the middle finger, squeezed with the index and ring fingers on each side, and pressed with the thumb on top (Figure 88A).

I prefer to grip a flying dart with my thumb pressing on the left groove (Figure 111).

THROWING A FLYING DART

The traditional target for flying darts is 6 feet tall and 7 inches wide. Seven circles are drawn on the target. The biggest circle has a diameter of six inches and has a 1.5-inch red heart inside; the smallest has a diameter of one inch and has a 0.3-inch red heart.

The flying dart can be thrown in two ways: with the palm facing up (positive hand) or with the palm facing down (negative hand) with spin or without spin. The positive hand throw on a dart that weighs more than 6 ounces is unique to the Chinese martial arts.

WITH SPIN THROW. The positive hand throw is not an easy throw and requires great wrist strength. Indeed, the development of wrist strength is part of the training for the positive hand throw. Chinese masters have developed their wrists such that they can throw flying darts accurately with the positive hand from as far as 40 feet.

The required wrist strength implies that the wrist bends at the time of release, which means that the dart will spin when thrown from 40 feet.

NO SPIN THROW. I tried throwing the flying dart with my palm facing up but I felt I did not have control over its release. I feel I have better control throwing it with the negative hand.

In my first throw, my dart stalled and hit sideways. On my ninetieth throw, I became aware of the dart's rotation along its longitudinal axis. I tried to duplicate it. Sometimes I was able to make the dart rotate along its longitudinal axis. At other times, it stalled. I was puzzled. After many throws, I found that when I pressed too hard on the left groove with my thumb, the dart stalled. When I decreased the pressure, the dart rotated along its longitudinal axis.

There is a simple explanation for this rotation. The clockwise (as viewed from the back of the thrower) rotation of a flying dart is imparted to it by the clockwise rotation of the throwing arm as it traces a circular arc. This rotation along its longitudinal axis is not necessary for the flying dart to stick, but it looks nice as it corkscrews toward the target.

The flying dart can only be thrown with no spin (a) from a close distance and (b) if the wrist is kept rigid at the time of release. Any bend in the wrist will cause the dart to spin.

It is very difficult to throw a flying dart with no spin. Indeed, in my first 100 throws I was able to stick a flying dart only four times.

I threw the dart from 17 feet. Since the experience was new to me, at the same time that I was trying to make it stick, I was studying its behavior in flight.

I used one 5-inch and two 6-inch flying darts to generate Figure 112. The two lengths throw equally well from 17 feet.

GOLDEN COIN DART

The golden coin dart as used in Chinese martial arts can be one of two kinds: a real coin used as money or a coin with sharp edges. They are both light. Even lighter are the coins with holes in the middle.

A sharp coin dart can deliver quite a sting. On the other hand, a light, dull-edged real coin will have to be thrown vigorously if it is to have an effect on the outcome of a fight. The golden coin dart may be replaced with a heavier coin-like implement, which can be made thicker to increase its potency as a throwing weapon.

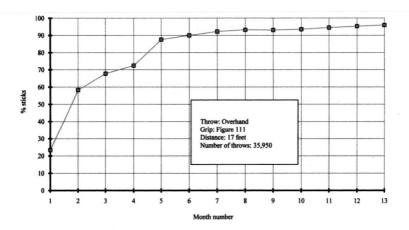

FIGURE 112.

My learning curve throwing a flying dart using the negative hand. I used a set of concentric circles, the outermost of which was 8" in diameter. I omitted the heart and substituted a circle with a diameter of 3". Rather than draw the circles, I pasted photocopies of the concentric circles on my cardboard targets.

FIGURE 113.

Coins that I throw. The 1⅛" diameter, ¹⁄₁₆" thick John F. Kennedy and Benjamin Franklin half-dollars are at the left. At the right is a coin-sized thrower I use as a substitute for a Chinese golden coin dart.

MAKING A GOLDEN COIN DART

I made ⅛" thick "coins" from steel plates. These coins are considerably thicker than the JFK half-dollar but of the same diameter. I made twenty coins because I expected to lose some since I throw on grass. To help locate them, I sprayed the coins with orange fluorescent paint.

I tapered the edge until it was nearly sharp. Sharp coins have to be carried in a special pouch as they can easily put holes in the pocket and, if accessed carelessly, can also easily cut fingers.

GRIPPING A GOLDEN COIN DART

A golden coin dart can be gripped between the thumb and index finger (Figure 114A). As many as three golden coin darts can be placed between the knuckles (Figure 114B) where the sharp edges just clear the inside of the palm.

A.

B.

C.

FIGURE 114.

Grips on a golden coin dart. Sharp-edged coins can be gripped between the thumb and the index finger (A) or between the knuckles (B). Coins with dull edges can be gripped in the manner shown in C, which is very much like the grip used on a baseball.

THROWING A GOLDEN COIN DART

Kungfu masters in the past favored throwing the golden coin dart with a positive hand. However, there is no reason why they cannot be thrown with a negative hand.

As many as four golden coin darts can be thrown simultaneously to ensure that the enemy is not able to avoid getting hit. It is for the same reason that the Philippine bagakays are thrown five at a time.

In throws using the grips in Figure 114A–B, coins will wobble toward the target and will seem to travel in slow motion. Nevertheless, these grips are good for close-quarter throws. From a greater distance, I prefer gripping dull-edged coins as in Figure 114C. With this grip, I am able to give a coin a vigorous rotation (which is needed) because it is very light.

You do not need to make your own golden coin darts. You can use the JFK half-dollar. However, make sure to coat the coin with bright paint. Otherwise, it will be difficult to find when you throw on grass.

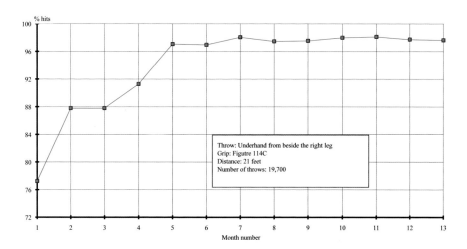

FIGURE 115.

My learning curve throwing the golden coin dart.

LEARNING CURVE CASE STUDY

The ideal target for a golden coin darts is clay or a mound of earth, because on impact, the coin will become embedded on such a target. However, it is not easy to set up a clay target. If you use an 8" circle pasted on cardboard, note that the coins will simply bounce off.

Golden coin darts can be thrown one or more at a time. When several are thrown at a time, an adversary can be hit even if he takes evasive action.

FLYING STEEL OLIVE

The steel olive was a very popular weapon among kungfu practitioners during the Ching and Ming Dynasties. Also known as the Chinese flying olive, they are shaped like a nut. Being pointed at both ends like a nail, they are also called nail-nuts. They are made of steel and are relatively heavy for their size of about 2½ inches long and with a diameter of about 1 inch. Since they are small, they are easily concealed. Several are normally carried in a bag.

FIGURE 116.

The steel olive I made is 2¼ inches long and has a ¾ inch diameter (left). At middle and right are two other throwers I made with square cross sections.

FIGURE 117.

Three-finger grip on a steel olive.

FIGURE 118.

You may obtain better control on the release of a steel olive by gripping it with four fingers.

MAKING A STEEL OLIVE

I bought a ¾" diameter 24"-long steel rod from a welding shop and cut it into 2¼"-long sections. Since I do not have a lathe, I tapered the two ends into a point using a file; then smoothed it all using a belt sander.

I made two other types of throwing implements that approximated the size of the traditional steel olive using ½" x ½" and 1" x 1" solid steel bars. These are shown in Figure 116.

Coat your steel olives with fluorescent paint because they can be easily lost on grass. Recoat the olives every so often as needed, to keep them visible.

GRIPPING A STEEL OLIVE

Kungfu practitioners hold the steel olive with the thumb, index finger, and middle finger (Figure 117). Try this grip; however, you may feel more comfortable with the grip shown in Figure 118 where I cradle the steel olive on my ring, middle, and index fingers and press it down with the thumb. The conical ends fit perfectly in my hand.

THROWING A STEEL OLIVE

The steel olive is short and stubby. As a defensive weapon, it is designed to disable by concussion. Though pointed at both ends, it cannot inflict the deep puncture wounds that a thin sharp knife or a flying sticker could. However, the $2\frac{1}{2}$"-long $\frac{1}{2}$" diameter steel olive is heavy enough to deliver a knockout blow.

I use eight layers of cardboard with no spaces between them when I throw wedge-like throwing implements such as knives or even bagakays. But steel olives thrown at such a target will simply bounce off it. Instead insert a crumpled piece of paper between the second and third layers thus creating space between them. With this arrangement, when the olive hits point first (or even sideways), it will become embedded on the target. Still, even with this modified target, the steel olive will often pop out of the target.

The ideal target for steel olives is clay or a mound of earth. However, if you do not have this kind of target, you'll need to replace the first two layers of cardboard (which will become mutilated after every twenty throws) frequently.

The steel olive can be thrown in such a way as to give it a pronounced rotation about its longitudinal axis (like the spin of a football). Or it can be made to spin end over end.

The number of spins that a knife, ax, or shuriken make as it speeds toward the target can be counted visually by an observer or with the help of a movie camera. Not so for the steel olive.

The steel olive spins end over end very fast. Hence, even if it hits point first, it will pop out of a cardboard target. However, while the desired result in throwing the steel olive is to make it hit the target point first, you may choose to make your goal a more modest one: to hit the designated target without regard to the olive's orientation at impact.

Throwing a steel olive is similar to throwing a ball or a stone. The stone does not have to stick to the target; it must merely hit the designated spot. For example: If my target measures $8\frac{1}{2}$" x 11", I count a throw as a hit if the steel olive makes an impact inside the lines.

LEARNING CURVE CASE STUDY

The steel olive will not stick on a cardboard target. Still, hitting the target will be a test of skill.

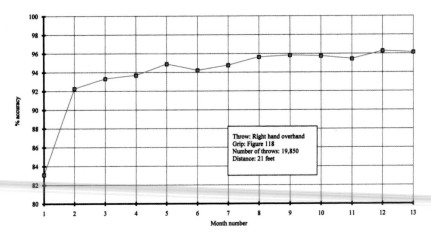

FIGURE 119.

My learning curve for throwing a steel olive. The target is 8½" wide and 11" tall

At one time, one of my students asked me, "If you are to carry a knife on your person, which one will it be?" My answer was, "I would rather bring the steel olive."

FLYING STICKER

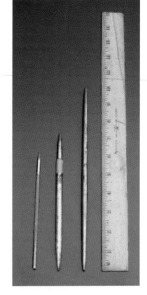

The Chinese flying sticker was created during the Ching Dynasty and was a popular weapon among kungfu fighters. It was an adaptation of a sticker used for fighting in water.

A flying sticker is cigar-shaped and sharp at both ends. It is 7" long and has a ¼" diameter. The 7-inch flying sticker is but a shorter version of the Philippine 10-inch bagakay. Being relatively light (about 6 ounces), twelve flying stickers are normally carried, hidden, on the shoulder or around the waist.

MAKING A FLYING STICKER

Flying stickers are not commercially available so you will have to make your own.

Buy ½ inch diameter steel rods from a hardware store and cut them into 7 inch lengths. Taper both

FIGURE 120.

The flying sticker (middle) is cigar-shaped but thinner. At left is a throwing needle with its tassel removed. At right is a 10" bagakay.

ends into 1½ inch tall cones using a bench grinder or a file. Smooth the cones using a belt sander or sandpaper. Do not make the points too sharp.

GRIPPING A FLYING STICKER

A sticker used for fighting in water has a ring at its middle. The middle finger is inserted in the ring to secure it; then the fingers are wrapped around its middle. This grip was carried over to the flying sticker.

A flying sticker has no ring since it was designed to be thrown. Still, it is held in the middle also (Figure 121).

What makes throwing a flying sticker unique is the location of the grip.

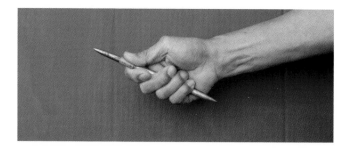

FIGURE 121.

A flying sticker is gripped in the middle with all fingers wrapped around it. About 1½ inch of its length protrudes past the bottom and top of the fist.

THROWING A FLYING STICKER

A flying sticker will stick on the target when it makes full spins. My first throwing distance for the two-pointed flying sticker is about 12 feet. From this distance, the sticker will complete one full spin and hit the target with its point (held initially toward the front). The second, third, or fourth throwing distance can be calculated using Equation 1, which was discussed in Chapter 1.

A flying sticker, because it is two-pointed, will also stick on the target when it makes half spins. My first throwing distance for the two-pointed flying sticker in the half spin throw is 8 feet. From this distance, the point of the sticker (the one initially held toward the thrower) will stick on the target. With an arm reach of 2 feet, my sticking distance is 6 feet.

The next (second farther) distance to throw it from to make it stick is 20 feet. This can be calculated from Equation 3 (page {X-REF}) using the given values of n (1), Z (6), and arm reach (2). From 20 feet, the sticker will make 1½ spins, and its point will hit the target.

LEARNING CURVE CASE STUDY

In the beginning, I was not comfortable throwing the flying sticker, and it showed in my sticking average. Sometimes, I would look at the embedded stickers and find that four hit the target after making 1½ spins. However, the fifth hit the target after making two full spins.

I had thought that I was throwing the sticker with consistency, so to find four hitting with 1½ spins and a fifth hitting with two full spins was exasperating. However, after 2,000 throws, I was able to consistently hit the target with flying stickers making 1½ spins only. At that time, I began to appreciate the merits of the grip.

It is apparent that this grip in the middle is very sensitive to small changes in sticking distance and in the location of the grip.

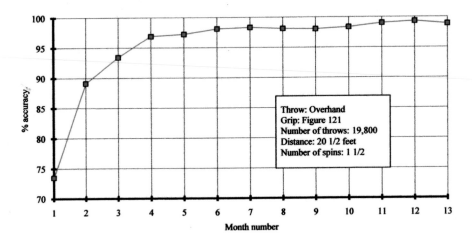

FIGURE 122.

My sticking percentage for the ¼" diameter, 7" long two-pointed flying sticker. To determine which end is hitting the target, I used orange tape on one end. I found this very helpful for checking my consistency. The target is 10" wide x 12" tall.

THE ART OF THROWING

- CHAPTER 5 -

OTHER THROWING
IMPLEMENTS

WESTERN DART

The Western dart is a very popular throwing implement. It is a light missile with an ingenious design.

Typically, a dart has a total length of 5" with a 2½" metal shaft with a needle-like tip. Attached (screwed) to it is a plastic tail with four vanes. The vanes function like the feathers of an arrow. They stabilize the dart in flight.

GRIPPING A WESTERN DART

I use two grips on the dart. In one, I squeeze it with my thumb on one side and with the index, middle and ring fingers at the opposite side (Figure 124A). In the other, I grip it only with my first three fingers (Figure 124B).

FIGURE 123.

A Western dart. Some darts have shorter vanes than others. Longer vanes will have noticeable curves that could affect your throwing average.

THROWING A WESTERN DART

It is not easy to throw an implement with no spin. However, at close distances the spin can be suppressed long enough until the implement hits the target. The most familiar no spin throwing implement is the spear. Still, the spear has to be held close to or at its CG to prevent it from spinning end over end. If the spear is gripped at the wrong location, it will still spin when thrown.

The very much shorter Japanese negishi-ryu shuriken can likewise be thrown with no spin. The spin is suppressed by applying downward pressure with the index finger (with the palm perpendicular to the ground) at the time of release. Additionally, horse or bear hair is attached to the tail of the negishi-ryu shuriken to stabilize it in flight and to prevent it from spinning.

The equally short Chinese flying dart can also be thrown with no spin. Its "Y" cross section makes it appear to have three vanes. However, because it is heavy, the vanes do not stabilize it in flight. The spin is suppressed by applying moderate pressure with the middle finger (by turning the palm down) at the time of release. Additionally, Chinese

A.

B.

FIGURE 124.

The four-finger (A) and three-finger (B) grips I use on a Western dart.

masters attach silk threads at its tail to stabilize it in flight and to prevent it from spinning.

The Japanese negishi-ryu shuriken and the Chinese flying dart have radically different shapes. Yet, if either is to be thrown with no spin, moderate pressure has to be applied at the time of release and/or there has to be a tail attachment.

On the other hand, it takes very little effort to throw a Western dart with no spin. Indeed, the no spin throw for a Western dart is effortless, thanks to the required attachment—the plastic tail with four vanes.

At close distances, the Western dart can be thrown with arm action only. However, from farther away, it has to be thrown like a knife where the twisting of the body reinforces the action of the arm. The arm action is very much like that in a baseball pitch.

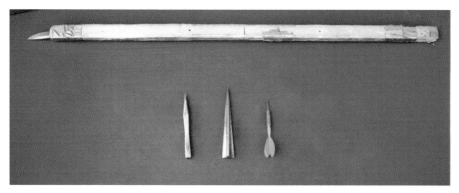

FIGURE 125.

Implements I throw with no spin: top, the spear; bottom (left to right), a Japanese negishi-ryu shuriken, a Chinese flying dart, and a Western dart. A Chinese steel olive can also be thrown with no spin.

It requires no effort to make a Western dart stick on the target. However, like other throwing implements, it has to be thrown with enough power to get to the target and with skill to hit what you are aiming at.

Damaged, loose, or curved vanes could affect your throwing average. To avoid damage to the vanes, use a maximum of five darts or use multiple targets (Figure 42). As an added precaution, when you hit the bull's-eye in your first throw, retrieve the dart immediately. From time to time, check to see if the vanes need to be tightened.

LEARNING CURVE CASE STUDY

A Western dart is normally thrown at a board that is partitioned in a number of ways. The throwing distance can be as close as 10 feet. Hence, throwing involves only the action of the arm.

There is no reason why a Western dart cannot be thrown from farther away. So I did.

BOOMERANG

Boomerangs are usually associated with Australian aborigines, although other peoples have also used them. There are two types of boomerangs: the returning, which is more of a plaything, and the non-returning, which is used in war.

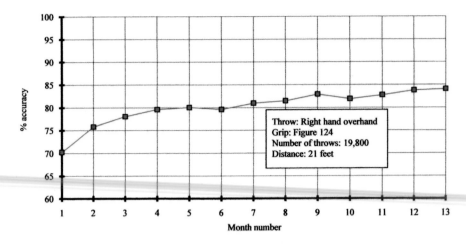

Throw: Right hand overhand
Grip: Figure 124
Number of throws: 19,800
Distance: 21 feet

FIGURE 126.

My percentage accuracy throwing a Western dart. The target is an 8½" x 11" sheet of paper.

The war boomerang or non-returning boomerang is designed to cut. They can be as long as 40 inches and sometimes even longer. This provides for the length of the fist with ample sharp length to cut a target with.

The returning boomerang is shorter—between 16 and 28 inches long. The arms are between 2" to 3" wide. The angle between the arms is between 70 and 120 degrees.

MAKING A BOOMERANG

I intended to throw a boomerang fifty times a day for thirteen months, so I had to make mine from steel plates. Wooden boomerangs will not withstand thirteen months of abuse.

I made three sizes of boomerangs from ⅛" thick steel plates (Figure 127). I kept the 1½" wide arms dull but

FIGURE 127.

The steel one-way boomerangs I fabricated have two sharp tips, a pointed vertex, and dull edges. The boomerangs measure, from tip to tip, (left to right) 6¼", 9½", and 10½". The angles between the arms are 90 degrees for the shorter boomerang and 120 degrees for the other two.

departed from the usual design by giving my version of the boomerang sharp tips.

It is easy enough to hit the target with any part of the boomerang. However, I wanted to throw mine such that it would puncture the target. Hence, I kept the edges dull and made the tips sharp.

The hardwood arms of boomerangs thrown by Australian aborigines are skewed by 2- or 3-degrees from the coplanar. This and the special technique of throwing it makes the boomerang return to its thrower.

I did not want a pointed boomerang to return after being thrown. Hence, I kept the arms coplanar.

I coated one of the arms with fluorescent paint because I wanted to know which arm was sticking on the target.

Gripping a boomerang

I use a knife-like grip on the boomerang (Figure 128) where I wrap my fingers around one of its arms.

Throwing a boomerang

I throw a non-returning boomerang on a vertical and sometimes on a diagonal. Throwing one is like throwing a crooked knife or an ax.

It is more difficult to throw a 90-degree boomerang than a 120-degree boomerang. If the release of the 90-degree boomerang is not timed correctly, it will hook on the palm and hit low. To compensate for the hooking action, throw

FIGURE 128.

The grip I use on a boomerang.

FIGURE 129.

The boomerang is heavy and will impact a target with authority.

the 90-degree boomerang on an arc higher than you would throw the equivalent straight knife. There is little hooking action with the 120-degree boomerang.

The boomerang will hit the target in a number of ways: with its 2 sharp tips, with its corner tip like an arrow without a shaft, and with the outside of its two arms. The inside of the arms can also hit the target, particularly when the angle between the arms is 120 degrees.

LEARNING CURVE CASE STUDY

It will take more skill to get a boomerang to stick on the target than to get it to cut with its sharp edges. With a sharp-tipped boomerang, I was able to count my sticking percentage and generate a learning curve; you can do the same.

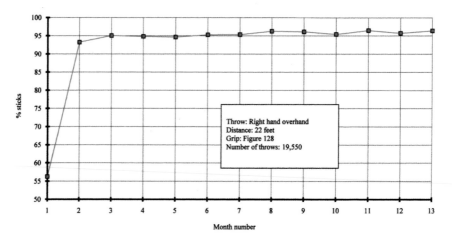

FIGURE 130.
My learning curve for throwing a boomerang. I used a 90-degree boomerang in the first month and hit only 56 percent. From the second month on, I used the 120 degree 10½" boomerang at which time there was a marked improvement in my sticking average. The target is an 8½" x 11" rectangle.

THE ART OF THROWING

- CHAPTER 6 -

SPORT AND DEFENSIVE THROWING

Skill will determine whether you will hit the target or not when throwing alone, in a sports competition, or in a defensive situation. However, in practice, the throwing distance is a known; this is not so when you face an enemy who could be moving. So, a defensive throw must be quick and must be disguised by some ruse.

In sport knife throwing, the target is fixed. You would have marked your throwing distance with a line on the ground or with a short visible stake. For a particular throw and for a particular knife, you will be throwing from the same distance each time. If you miss the bull's-eye, your target will still be there the next day.

The requirements in sport knife throwing are more stringent. Your knife will have to stick on the target to get counted.

The desired effect of a defensive knife throw is also to make the knife stick on the target. However, even if a thrown knife hits flat or butt first, the throw would still "count." A throw that hits flat could still knock out the enemy. A throw that misses the nose but instead hits the eyes will inflict a more serious injury. A throw that merely grazes could make the enemy blink, thus, giving the thrower the time to make a getaway or to advance.

In sport knife throwing, you throw for points. In defensive knife throwing, you throw for keeps.

STICK FIGHTING, KNIFE FIGHTING, AND KNIFE THROWING

I consider knife throwing an integral part of stick and knife fighting. All stick and knife fighting techniques are throwing actions. For example: Strike downward with a stick. At the same time, open up your fingers. Do the same with a knife. The stick and the knife will fly away from your hands.

I had a student who attended stick and knife fighting classes for two years. In the twenty-third and twenty-fourth months, I decided that it was time for him to throw knives. I handed him my throwing knives and said, "Go ahead. Throw." His knives stuck. He was surprised, but I was not. Stick fighting and knife fighting prepared him for knife throwing.

WHY THROW AN IMPLEMENT?

Why should you throw a knife? If you miss, you would have lost your weapon.

Instinct will predispose a skilled thrower to pick up any object when there is a need for a defensive throw. The object that one could throw in a self-defense situation does not have to be a knife. It can be a can of sardines, a stone, an apple, or a tomato. Or a chair. Or sand. It is easier to hit a target with such objects because one need not be concerned about its orientation at contact. Any way a can of sardines hits, it is going to hurt—never mind a chair!

WHY LEARN MORE THAN ONE THROW?

For defensive knife throwing, you need to have more than one option. For example: Picture yourself in a situation where the adversary is crouched under a table. Your vertical or diagonal overhand throw will not get to him. Even a near-horizontal throw might not get to him. Similarly, outdoors, low tree branches will interfere with your overhand throw. Obviously, these situations require the use of an underhand throw.

However, if you were in knee-deep water or surrounded by knee-high reeds, you might not be able to throw underhand. You would be cutting water or grass with your throwing knife. In both instances, you have to throw overhand.

—◆—

THROWING
IMPLEMENTS AND
YOUR HANDS

If you practice throwing only occasionally, you might take the care of your hands for granted. However, if you practice on a regular basis, your fingers can be rubbed raw by repeated throws. For this reason, the throwing implement must be (a) modified if needed and (b) kept clean, sharp, and repaired before and after use. The liberal use of duct tape will provide added protection. In winter, you will need to wear gloves.

MODIFYING THE BLADE OR THE HANDLE

Throwing implements such as knives, bagakays, axes, spears, shurikens, and shakens are not cheap. Some can also cut your fingers. For these reasons, you might need to modify them.

Doubled-edged throwing knives are designed to be thrown by the handle. If you want to throw them by the blade, the edges can be dulled on a bench grinder or by filing.

Knives with serrated backs, such as the AK-47 bayonet and the K-Bar can be thrown by the blade. Though the serration is not sharp, constant rubbing against your fingers at the time of release will cut your skin raw. To protect your hands, grind out the serration or put tape on it.

TAPING THE HANDLE

Taping the handle is almost necessary for knives that have plastic, rubber, or wooden scales. This will prevent the handle from chipping, or worse, splitting.

Taping is needed even more for the handle of the AK-47 bayonet. It is attached to a gun through deep grooves underneath its handle. To protect your hands, wrap the handle with two layers of duct tape. Make sure to tape the handle working toward the blade so that your fingers will not catch on the edges of the tape as you release the knife.

ADDING WEIGHT

You can increase the weight of a knife by wrapping several layers of duct tape on the handle. Of course, this will change the location of its CG and will change the behavior of the knife. I resort to this method to increase the weight of 4-ounce knives for throwing underhand.

MAKING THE IMPLEMENT MORE VISIBLE

Short lengths of orange electrical tape or a coat of fluorescent paint will make implements more visible when you throw on grass.

To avoid losing throwing implements, retrieve them immediately after a particularly bad throw. If you throw several more after a bad throw, you will not remember where to look for the errant implement. Also, if you do not retrieve it immediately, it will become mental clutter.

The most difficult weapons to find are the cigar-shaped steel bagakays, which can easily be lost in the grass. A metal detector is a good tool for finding lost knives, but a heavy magnet from a hardware store works just as well and costs under $20. It will literally suck up the lost knife. You would not want to mow your lawn with a lost knife in your yard!

CARE OF YOUR THROWING IMPLEMENTS

Bring a fine file and a roll of duct tape to your throwing sessions.

The care of your throwing implements after use should become a matter of routine. It will extend their useful life, prevent cuts on your fingers, ensure many successful throws, and avoid the risk of a really bad throw.

If you hit an already embedded implement with another, retrieve both immediately. Run your fingers very lightly on them to check for nicks. Smooth any nick using a fine file, then remove any burr using sandpaper.

After you throw, clean all your implements with detergent to remove dirt, grass, or leaves. Apply the detergent with a sponge. Wipe the implement dry with a paper towel or a piece of cloth.

Check the tips for bends or chips. Hammer any bend using sharp, light taps over an anvil. Sharpen chipped tips with a file or on a bench grinder.

The wooden shaft of a spear will become chipped when hit by a subsequent throw. To prevent splinters from getting into your hands, smooth any chip with a file then put duct tape over it.

Many throwing implements, particularly knives, are made from stainless steel. However, there are many good throwing knives that are not rustproof. (You would be surprised at how fast some of these knives rust.) To remove thin layers of rust, use rust "erasers" which cost about $5. The axes, knives, bagakays, shurikens, shakens, flying darts, steel olives, and disks (coins) that I designed and fabricated are not rustproof. Hence, I put my rust "erasers" to good use.

Prevention is the best way of taking care of your throwing implements. To minimize the possibility of hitting an already embedded implement, I use a wide target that is 4-foot wide by 3-foot high. I partition this into smaller sections either by drawing a 12" wide by 14" tall rectangle or pasting images printed on 8½" by 11" paper on the target board. In this way, I am able to direct my subsequent throws to a still hole-free part of the board.

In precision throwing, when I hit the center of the target, I retrieve the implement immediately.

CARE OF YOUR HANDS

If you throw a heavy all-metal ax, say, 100 times in one practice session everyday, the repeated throws will rub your thumb, index finger, and middle finger raw. To avoid losing your fingerprints, you can wrap two layers of duct tape on those fingers (Figure 131). One layer of duct tape wrapped around the handle of the ax will give you added protection. The duct tape on the handle, aside from protecting your skin, will also help prevent nicks on your ax. If you only throw occasionally, you will not need the duct tape.

You can also wrap the handles of your throwing knives with duct tape. However, you do not need to wrap tape on your fingers when you throw lighter throwing implements. You will experience a certain degree of discomfort in the beginning, but as you throw more, you will get used to the duct tape.

Eventually, abrasion will expose the glue and will make the duct tape sticky. When this happens retape the implement. If you do not have tape on hand, rub dirt on it—and clean it after practice.

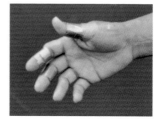

FIGURE 131.

Duct tape on the index finger, thumb, and middle finger. Do not use more than two layers of duct tape. If you do, you will not be able to bend your fingers.

CONCLUSION: ART, THEORY, AND PRACTICE

As mentioned in previous chapters there are many variables involved in a throw. These include

Physical
    Knife (or any implement)
    Grip
        Blade – there are a number of blade grips that can be used on a knife
        Handle – there are a number of handle grips that can be used on a knife
    Distance
    Type of throw: underhand or overhand
Physical, personal
    Physical condition
    Mechanics of the throw
Mental
    Mental clutter

If one is to make a knife stick, the number of *physical variables* must be kept to a minimum—ideally to zero. For example: One can throw ten identical knives, using the same grip, throwing from the same distance, and using the overhand throw. Thus, one has only two other variables to contend with: *physical (personal)* and *mental.*

You might be in good physical condition. Still, there are variables that could affect your throw. During the backward swing of your arm, you might inhale a lungful of exhaust fumes from a passing car. Of course, when you throw in a forest such a thing will not happen. Still, there could be mental clutter such as sound that breaks the silence or movement that suddenly appears in the corner of your eye.

In theory, if the thrower is to stick his knife when gripped by the blade, he should throw such that Equation 3 is satisfied.

$$\text{Throwing distance} = (2n + 1)Z + \text{Arm reach}$$

In practice, you can make a beginning thrower put his front toe on the exact spot for the throwing distance, you can give him a specific knife, and give him all sorts of instructions, but still he will not stick the knife consistently. If the beginner sticks the knife, it is more because of luck. Why?

There is more to the knife throw than meets the eye. There are variables that we cannot assign a number to and that do not show up in Equation 3.

We can represent a knife throw with a more complex equation that will determine not only throwing distance, but whether or not the knife will stick.

$$\begin{aligned} \text{Good throw} = {}&\text{Must satisfy Equation 3} \\ &+ \text{Zero physical variable} \\ &+ \text{Zero mental clutter} \\ &+ \text{Consistent (constant) mechanics of the throw} \end{aligned}$$

It is difficult not to have mental clutter when you throw. Lack of confidence is mental clutter. So are personal problems. However, with practice, the thrower can reduce mental clutter and can reach a mental state where he is able to "empty his mind"—where he is able to isolate his *self* from the rest of the universe.

You can keep records, compute your accuracy percentage and generate a learning curve of your throws. In that way, you can measure your accuracy and express it with a number. On the other hand, one cannot assign a number to how "empty" the mind is nor can one assign a number to the consistency of the mechanics of his throw. These two variables are intricately linked—one cannot be separated from the other. However, a manifestation of this link is observable.

Art, form, the smoothness of the throwing motion, results when the mechanics of the throw is mastered, when the mind is emptied—and when the knife sticks.

EPILOGUE: THE NAIL

I went to high school in Manila where my family had a small store. I would help at the store very early in the morning and after classes in the afternoon.

We sold grapes that were packed in sawdust inside wooden boxes. My father would open the box, pull out bunches of grapes and place them on the counter. Occasionally, there would be a grape or two that became detached from the bunch. I made a game of searching for them by touch in the sawdust. Those were the sweetest grapes I ever tasted.

Beyond the selling of grapes, my father also found use for the packing materials. The sawdust supplemented the wooden fuel that we cooked with. He would also pull out the nails from the wooden box and pile the wood neatly in a corner. He brought the bent nails home—for me to make straight. While I would have rather read books, I never complained about the chore. At the time, I did not realize that I was being given the *most important lesson of my life. I had to straighten the nails. I had to extract one more use from them.*

We sold a number of other things. Some we wrapped in old newspapers. However, *before the newspapers became wrappers, I read them and solved all the crossword puzzles I found.* Hence, I extracted one more use from the newspapers. I was able to make one more nail straight.

I could have concluded this book with the chapter "My Throwing Implements." Obviously, I didn't—because I had one more nail to make straight. I had to learn one more aspect of throwing. There was still part of my brain I had not used; there was still an arm movement I had not done; there was one more throw I had to learn so I added the chapter "Japanese Throwing Implements." To complete that chapter, I threw the shaken and the shuriken a total of 167,250 times.

I could not stop even then, though, as it didn't feel right to exclude Chinese throwing implements. I had one more nail to make straight, so I extended my self-imposed deadline. After 95,550 throws, I completed the chapter on Chinese throwing implements.

There were aches and pains along the way both physically and mentally. Over the fourteen years it took me to complete my goals, I experienced pain in my wrists, fingers, elbows, knees, ankles, soles, and toes. And head too. Worst, there was a time when my eyes started going bad. I did not stop throwing my knives, though. I still kept score using the sound of the impact of the knife on my target to determine whether the knife hit point first or not. A knife that hits with its point first will make little noise—a dull thud. One that does not sounds, to me, like a thunderclap. Fortunately, after two eye operations, I have good eyesight again.

I threw the implements when it was very hot, when it was very cold, when there was snow on the ground, when it was drizzling, when I was sneezing, when I had a fever, when I was hobbling, when I was feeling lazy, and even when I had a heavy heart. I could have stopped but for one more nail.

I had planned to complete this work three chapters earlier, but I couldn't. There was still a grip I hadn't used and implements I hadn't thrown. I had to extract one more use from my arm. *It is a nail I had to make straight—one more time.*

APPENDIX A

RULES OF COMPETITION
FOR KNIFE AND AX THROWING

These are the rules I use for my students. These rules are self-defense oriented since my students are allowed only a few tries to find their throwing distances.

The throwing area must be secured to ensure the safety of the competitors and spectators.

THROWING DISTANCE. The throwing distance must be at least 16 feet. The contestant will be allowed three practice throws to determine his throwing distance. He will also be allowed to mark it.

NUMBER OF THROWS TO QUALIFY IN THE FINALS. Each contestant will throw five consecutive times of which three must stick to qualify for the finals.

NUMBER OF THROWS IN THE FINALS. Each contestant who qualifies for the finals will throw five times.

TARGET IN THE FINALS. The target will consist of concentric circles with a maximum diameter of 8 inches and a minimum diameter of 2 inches.

THE WINNER. The winner will be the contestant with the most sticks.

In case of a tie, each contestant will be allowed one additional throw. The contestant who sticks his knife closest to the center of the target will be declared the winner.

Rules used in the European Knife Throwing and Ax Throwing Championships

Standard Events	Minimum Distance, meters	Number of Throws for Each Distance*
Knife blade rigid length: longer than 23cm width: narrower than 6 cm	3, 5, 7	21
Ax weight: min 290 g blade breadth: max 12 cm	4, 7	21
Long Distance	7	3

* In case of bad weather, time constraints or other emergency situations, the organizer can decide to limit throwers to only 15 throws.

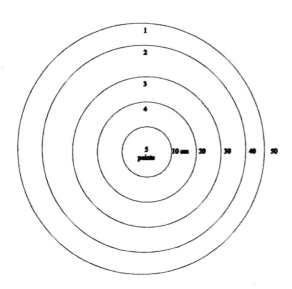

FIGURE A1

Dimensions of targets used in European Knife and Ax Throwing Championships

Spin	Minimum Distance, feet	Number of Throws for Each Distance
½	8	5
1	11	5
1½	15	5
2	18	5
2½	21	5
3	24	5

Knives must be no shorter than 12 inches, no longer than 16 inches, and must have a point on only one end. One set of knives, of uniform shape, material and weight, must be used for the competition.

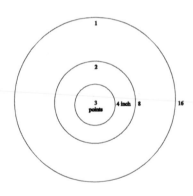

FIGURE A2

Dimensions of targets used in IKTHOF competitions—The 5 knives must be thrown in a "W" pattern. (For convenience, the targets are numbered.) The knives must stick in the sequence 1, 2, 3, 4, and 5 to be counted. The targets are cross sections of logs.

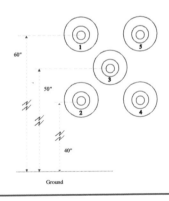

APPENDIX B

LINEAR AND ANGULAR SPEEDS
OF A THROWING IMPLEMENT

A point on a rotating object located at distance R from the axis of rotation traces a circle of radius R. For example: In knife throwing, the rotating object is the knife held in the hand, the point is any point in the knife such as its CG or its tip, and the axis of rotation is the thrower's shoulder.

The CG of the knife will have both linear speed (V) and angular speed (w) which are defined as

$$V = \frac{\text{total distance traveled}}{\text{time interval}}$$

$$w = \frac{\text{angle traversed}}{\text{time interval}}$$

Angular speed (degrees/second or radians/second) is one of two ways to measure the rate of rotation. The other is angular frequency (f) which is defined as

$$f = \frac{\text{number of revolutions}}{\text{time interval}}$$

The unit of frequency (f) is revolutions/second or revolutions/minute.

Linear speed and angular speed are related by the equation

$$V = w\text{R}$$

which means that any point on the knife farther away from the shoulder will have a greater linear speed. Consider Figure 132.

The knife is held with its CG a distance r away from the shoulder. When released, it will have a linear speed of v, that is,

$$v = w\text{r}$$

If the knife is held such that its CG is farther away from the shoulder at a distance R, it will have a greater linear speed V (with w held constant), that is,

$$V > v$$

For example: The CG of a shuriken held in the jikishin grip (Figure 88B) is closer to the axis of rotation (the shoulder joint) than when the shuriken is held as in Figure 91D. Thus, held as in Figure 91D, the shuriken when thrown will spin faster and will complete one full spin quicker. For this reason, for an equal number of spins, you will have to be farther from the target when you use Figure 88B than when you use Figure 91D.

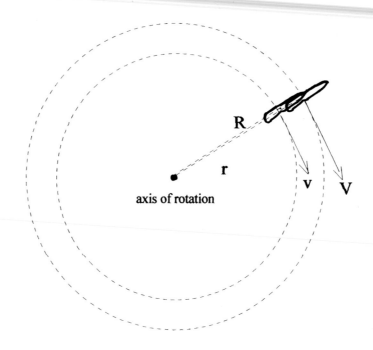

FIGURE 132.

The center of the circle is the axis of rotation, which is the knife thrower's shoulder. (Not drawn to scale.)

APPENDIX C

PERSONALITIES OF THE THROWING ARTS

They are all knife throwers, promoters of the sport and performers on stage, television, and movies. They represent a cross section of the knife throwing world.

Some would only throw a knife at a target. Others take a dim view of combat throwing while a few would practice only combat knife throwing.

Those who do shows and perform on stage aim around their human targets; others who compete in knife/ax/tomahawk throwing aim to hit the bull's-eye.

Some would only throw heavy knives; others prefer to throw light shurikens.

Many in the beginning were self-taught until they found the internet, DVDs, or books. Michael Bainton started with great instructors. Dalmo Mariano Da Silva couldn't; he was all alone in Brazil. Others, like Dalmo, had to learn by trial and error.

Many competed in tournaments. Others didn't.

Houzan Suzuki throws no-spin from as far as 18 meters. Roy Hutchison considers the no-spin throw as not fun but hard work. Scott Gracia looks at the no-spin throw as "cool," but sticks to the overhand with-spin throw that he knows best.

Some have taught hundreds of students. Others enable throwers from all over the world to learn from their websites.

Most will mark their throwing distances. Others delight in throwing from any distance.

Many are members of the six major associations in the United States active in promoting the sport and art of throwing. Chris Kelly, Houzan Suzuki, and Ralph Thorn are members of the World Association of Weapons Throwers (WAWT), which has no physical base except a website. Jeff Adams throws alone.

TABLE C1. Associations in the US active in promoting the sport and art of throwing

American Knife Throwers Alliance	AKTA
International Knife Throwers Alliance	IKTA
International Knife Throwers Hall of Fame	IKTHOF
Pacific Knife Throwers	PKT
Wild West Arts Club	WWAC
World Federated Knife Throwers	WFKT
World Knife Throwers Guild	WKTG

In the US, the associations have their own throwing rules. In Europe, each country had their own, but in September 2008, several European countries came to an agreement on a standard set of rules.

Despite their different perspectives on knife throwing and their individual styles, they all have some things in common. They are all dedicated, they all love throwing, they all would like to see the continued growth of the sport and art of throwing.

For lack of a better word, I used "personality" as a collective name for those whose profiles appear here. They are featured alphabetically except for Che Che White Cloud who started throwing at the age of 5 and who became a professional at age 7.

TABLE C2. Places of birth and citizenships of the profiled personalities

Personality	Place of birth	Citizenship
Todd Abrams	US	American
Rev. Dr. Adam R. Adamovich	US	American
Jeffrey D. Adams	US	American
John L. Bailey	US	American
Dr. Michael J. Bainton	England	American
Bobby Branton	US	American
Joseph Darrah	US	American
Scott D. Gracia	US	American
Richard L. Haines	US	American
Roy Hutchison	England	English
Chris S. Kelly	US	American
Cynthia Morrison	US	American
Michael Pahl	Germany	German
Kenneth Pierce	US	American
Dalmo Mariano Da Silva	Brazil	Brazilian
Houzan Suzuki	Japan	Japanese
John Taylor	England	English
Christian Thiel	Germany	German
Eric Ralph Thornburg	US	American

KENNETH PIERCE

CHE CHE WHITE CLOUD: A LIVING LEGEND

His knives were made from circular saw blades and were used by Kenneth Pierce's great grandfather for 48 years. His father used them for 67 years and he had used them for 64 years. The knives were originally 16" long but now they are only 12". During the time that the knives became shorter by 4 inches, at the rate of 0.0223 inches a year, the family made history.

Che Che White Cloud was born Kenneth Pierce. He spent his boyhood days at Shongo, New York on the Seneca Indian reservation located near the present day Salamanca, New York. He is of mixed Seneca and Onondaga blood of the Hodenosaunee of the Six Nations of the Iroquois Confederacy. The Pierce bloodline can be traced back into Native American history for 10 generations.

FIGURE 133.

The White Clouds. Che Che White Cloud was inducted into the IKTHOF in 2004 as the Outstanding Knife Thrower of the 20th Century.

FIGURE 134.

Recent pictures of Che Che White Cloud with Joe "Brokenfeather" Darrah holding Che Che White Cloud's throwing knives.

His grandfather toured with the Wild West shows in the 1800s. His father Chief White Cloud traveled with Buffalo Bill's Wild West Show. Che Che White Cloud came from a long line of warriors skilled in the art of war—throwing the spear, shooting the bow and arrow, and throwing knives and tomahawks.

At the age of 5, Che Che suffered a serious injury in his right arm that was caught in an old wringer washer. His arm muscles were re-attached by a German physician who was a friend of the family. Facing the prospects of a long rehabilitation, his father made him squeeze putty then rubber balls. His father went on with the therapy that included exercises that helped Che Che regain the normal range of motions of a healthy arm. One of the exercises is that of the throwing motion.

Che Che's family had been entertaining for over 200 years when he got hurt. Che Che was next in line to his father and did not need much urging to practice throwing, eight hours a day, everyday. After two years, he became so good that he turned professional at age seven. In his early teens he was recognized as the world's finest thrower, but he was just getting started. Soon he became the star of the show using rifles, pistols, bow & arrows, blowguns, knives, tomahawks, and many other one of a kind impalement items that were designed by his father or his family such as the Butterfly Axe that Larry Cisewski throws in his act.

He has appeared and thrown knives, shot arrows, and thrown spears in many movies. He threw a spear at Clark Gable in the movie Mogambo, he threw knives in the movie The Iron Mistress with Alan Ladd, he tacked Lucille Ball to the wall, he worked with Clayton Moore (The Lone Ranger), and he also worked with Lash LaRue, Sonya Hennie, Gene Autry, Will Rogers and many other famous celebrities.

Joe Darrah is a very close friend of Che Che. In one of their discussions, Joe recalls, "Che Che told me that this was an art form and that just as in building a house your foundation was your feet and that is where you throw from. The slightest difference in your stance when setting your base could have a different outcome and if your feet weren't right it could mean the difference between an extraordinary show and one where your target girl was left wounded, so always throw from your feet." Che Che often retied his moccasins three or four times until they felt right and then he would throw. Aspiring knife throwers were watching Che Che's hands, they should have been watching his feet!

In one of his performances, Che Che would shoot arrows and blowgun darts to outline his mother then his wife, and then the spectators are primed for his knife throwing. He throws from 9 feet, nine half-pound knives one to the left and one to the right until all his knives encircle his smiling assistant—his wife Donna—in exactly three seconds! His knives were so close to Donna, a direct descendant of Daniel Boone, that the knives have first to be removed before she can move away.

Che Che White Cloud had elevated his Art into a science. Joe continues, "I consider him to be the best knife thrower ever but he is very unassuming and a bit cantankerous if he doesn't know you and slightly prejudiced against what the white man has done to the Native American peoples but when asked who he thinks could ever out throw him the answer is always the same 'my Father was the best thrower in the world' and while I never had the opportunity to see his father throw, except in a few early westerns, I find it hard to believe anyone could surpass what I've seen Che Che do with a knife!!!"

Che Che has been given somewhere between 75 and 100 plaques, citations, and awards in his lifetime. His family believes that he is the only Native American to have been inducted into the Cowboy Hall Of Fame. Che Che White Cloud was inducted into the IKTHOF in 2003 for International Achievement and in 2004 as the Outstanding Knife Thrower of the 20th Century.

Che Che's only aim these days is to teach about the old ways and help the young people to learn the old arts.

TODD ABRAMS
JACK DAGGER

When asked about his start, Todd says, "I was originally self-taught. Then, once I entered competition, I experienced what I refer to as 'osmotic learning'—picking up good habits from great throwers. Eventually, I spent several weeks with Mike 'Alamo' Bainton, refining my throwing style, and drilled everything into my muscle memory intensively."

Todd has been throwing most of his life—ever since he was old enough to own a pocket knife—about twenty-two years. Todd started throwing in the early eighties using screwdrivers. He bought his first throwing ax and tomahawk in 1988. Eventually he purchased his first proper throwing knife from the late Harry McEvoy in 1990.

Todd has a generous streak in him. Todd collects whatever books he comes across, occasional video (DVDs), and has a moderate collection of throwing implements. "Moderate because," he says, "I have a bad habit of giving my throwers away to promising students as they come along."

The lightest weapons that Todd ever threw were 4" long steel cocktail skewers that hardly weighed anything at all. He recalls, "When I was still bartending, I taught my colleagues how to throw those into boxes and sheetrock, much to

FIGURE 135 (FAR LEFT).

Todd throws his knife in practice. (Photo by John Leonetti).

FIGURE 136 (LEFT).

Todd just before he goes on stage to throw around his human target.

the dismay of my employers." The heaviest weapon that Todd threw was his first throwing axe which he still owns and has fondly christened "Trogdor." It's a seven-pound, one-handed thrower. According to Todd, "Trogdor is a beast."

Todd throws half-spin from as close as 1 foot and as far as 40 feet; full-spin from 3 feet and 50 feet and no-spin from 15 feet. And he will throw them all. He says, "Throwing is fun! If my keyboard had a point, I'd throw it right now."

Todd, at the start, was a recreational backyard thrower. He organized the Baton Rouge Knife and Axe Throwers Club. Many of his students were very young, and he teaches knife throwing as a fun, safe, confidence building exercise. He does not throw in a backyard anymore, as he moved to Los Angeles in 2003. He lives in an apartment with no backyard but teaches as often as he can either at a park nearby or at his good friend Anthony DeLongis' Rancho Indalo.

"Working" to Todd, is throwing around a person on stage, and making the audience laugh. After an injury Todd had to learn to throw left handed for about three months before he could resume throwing right handed. He must have been the only knife throwing performer who's ever performed his entire show with his non-dominant hand. Todd is "Jack Dagger, The King of Fling" when working.

Todd also performs as "Jergen" in The Van Kleaver Bros Comedy Dutch Chef Knife Throwing Show (in the Renaissance Faire circuit) for which he designed and utilizes the world's only "Throwing Spatula."

Todd's first television commercial had him throwing a tomahawk at a Louisiana-shaped target covered in bacon; a bizarre campaign ad for a Baton Rouge lawyer's campaign for Lieutenant Governor. Since he moved to Los Angeles, Todd has performed in hundreds of shows and made several television appearances (including Japanese and Greek television). He has appeared in the TV series Monk as a Zemenian Chef, as a tech advisor and stunt thrower in Fox's Bones, as himself in History Channel's More Extreme Marksmen, and as Adam Sandler's stunt hands in You Don't Mess with the Zohan.

Todd is a member of the IKTHOF and used to compete very often. He won several national championships and once set a world record in speed throwing. He doesn't compete anymore but helps run or emcee throwing events as frequently as his work schedule permits. He says, "I think it's very important for any thrower to attend, and participate in, as many tournaments as possible."

Todd does outdoor shows even in near-freezing temperatures. In one such show in 2006, he recalls, "My knives were so cold, it was like throwing icicles. Pretty soon I couldn't feel my hands. I was able to throw the knives where I wanted them to go, but I couldn't always get them to rotate correctly, so I was dropping a few here and there. At some point, I just had to laugh. It wasn't a safety issue or I would've stopped the show, but I just thought it was funny. A cute security guard brought me a hot water bottle which I wrapped in a towel and kept on top of my knives to keep them from freezing. Worked like a charm. I still have that damn hot water bottle!"

Todd was inducted into the IKTHOF as Impalement Artist of the Year in 2005, as National Knife Throwing Entertainer of the Year in 2006, and for International Achievement and Promotion of Knife Throwing in 2008.

DAVID R. ADAMOVICH, PH. D.
(THE GREAT THROWDINI)

David Adamovich is a man of letters, having a doctorate in exercise physiology from Teacher's College at Columbia University. He taught electrocardiography at university level for 18 years. His students addressed him as "Prof. Dr. Adamovich."

Dr. Adamovich is also a man of the cloth, having studied theology at the Unity in Christ Christian Fellowship Ministry. As an ordained minister, he's officiated at more than 3,000 wedding ceremonies. The bride and groom address him as "The Reverend Dr. Adamovich."

The Rev. Dr. Adamovich is also a Man of Steel—knives, that is—being an impalement artist extraordinaire. The audience in his shows and performances know him as The Great Throwdini.

David started throwing late in life—at the age of 50. (He is now 62.) He competed for the first five years. In his first competition, the tournament organizer told everyone to stop and take notice of David's throwing style, "Now that's the smoothest knife thrower I've ever seen," said Bob Karp. In five years of competition he's placed first in three major knife throwing events: the AKTA Nationals (novice), and both the IKTA and WFKT World Championships. Afterward, he turned to the stage and is now in his twelfth year of throwing and his seventh year as a professional knife thrower.

FIGURE 137.

One of The Great Throwdini's most prominent contributions to the impalement arts was introducing audiences to the formal attire associated with Vaudeville of the 1930s.

With a kick-start from Harry Munroe, The Northeast knife throwing champion, David took off on a rapid self-taught program to quench his thirst for the scientific basis of knife throwing. Subsequently he produced *The Fundamentals of Knife, Hawk and Axe Throwing with an Introduction to the Impalement Arts* (book and DVD) and coauthored *A Day on Broadway*, which relives his experience about first performing The Wheel of Death on stage from his perspective and that of the target girl Astrid.

The Great Throwdini throws knives for half-spins from around 7 feet and tomahawks, axes, and machetes full-spins from 12 feet. He says, "A simple straightforward overhand half-spin throw is the standard throw in the impalement arts. It's our bread and butter throw." In one of his stunts, he throws with both hands putting five knives in each of his front pockets and throws them alternating, Ladder of Death fashion, on opposite sides of his partner.

As an impalement artist, he uses a 4 foot wide by 6 foot high flat board (versus target rounds) and a 6 foot diameter Wheel of Death. Noted for the speed of his throwing, Throwdini has been videotaped throwing 2 knives per second at the spinning wheel. He has one piece of advice to aspiring impalement artists, "Practice, practice, practice, and if you use human targets then aim to miss—they'll last longer that way!"

Clearly "The World's Fastest and Most Accurate Knife Thrower," he's set and broken 20 worlds records. Among them the most knives (144) thrown around a human target in one minute, the fastest time (4.00 seconds) to throw a 10 knife Ladder of Death around a human target, and the fastest time (3.73 seconds) to throw 10 knives. One of his records has been acclaimed as "One of The Top 100 Guinness World Records of All Time." As for accuracy, he's cut the ashes off a lit cigarette just 2 inches from the nose of his target girl (wife, Barbara) without touching the cigarette. All of his records are performed with 14" professional Throwdini Throwers.

The Great Throwdini also holds the world record for the most knives (25) caught in one minute, but it came with a price. A knife went through his hand in an attempt to break that record. No major damage was done, however, and he performed his act with a bandaged hand just several hours later. He is the first and only person to have performed the Triple Crown: the bullet, arrow, and knife catch. Others have performed one, maybe two, but he made history as the first person to have performed all three dangerous projectile catches.

He has traveled the world and performed on many high-profile TV shows but TV is not his only conquest. Throwdini has authored and/or been written about in: *A Day on Broadway*, *The Guinness Book of World Records*, *Ripley's Expect the Unexpected*, *American Sideshow*, *The Daredevil's Manual*, and *Spectacle Circus* magazine. He has even created and produced the Off-Broadway sensation, "Maximum Risk - World Champions on The Edge!"

Throwdini has developed several knife throwing stunts: the Knife-Catch, the Double Ladder of Death, and the Card-Stab. His act includes tight and fast throwing of knives, tomahawks, and axes around a target girl, throwing with both hands, throwing blindfolded, speed throwing, throwing through a paper-veil to a strobe light, and The Wheel of Death.

He's worked with several partners—all alive and well—depending on venue and availability. The most famous, Target Girl Tina, is a professional belly dancer and bull whip artist as well. Together they blend their talents to "tell a story" from first to last knife. When one Target Girl was asked about the worst thing that ever happened, she said, "He forgot his lines." When asked if he's ever going to slow down, he replied, "I just keep getting faster."

JEFFREY D. ADAMS

In regards to his throwing weapon of choice, the dart that Jeff Adams uses is different from the delta shape one that the author made. "Mine is 5 inches long $\frac{5}{16}$ inch across, hexagonal and difficult at first to throw. I spent three years experimenting with different shapes and sizes and this is what I came up with. I practice regularly (weather permitting) out to about 18 feet but I have been successful out to 30 feet. The dart is very light and rough on the joints and muscles initially but highly concealable. At this stage of the game, I can deal with it fine." Pain comes with the territory.

Jeff continued, "About two weeks ago, the weather was good enough to practice. So after three months of not throwing, I went out and made 31 good throws before I had a miss. With my technique, I find at the longer distances, one of the most important factors is maintaining the channel formed by your fingers as discussed in Douglas Shieh's *Ancient Chinese Hidden Weapons*. Also I have found it is important to raise your elbow up. The elbow comes up and back then your hand comes back and your elbow comes forward followed by

FIGURE 138.

Jeff throwing his darts

your hand and the release. Some people have called it a whipping motion."

Jeff's target for his darts are 2 inch diameter red dots painted from top to bottom of a 2" by 12" by 8' long plank. He also practices throwing at a plank laid on the ground to his front to simulate the top of someone's foot. By throwing at this area it can surprise/incapacitate an opponent. Sometimes, he simply leans an unmarked panel of wood against the side of a barn and throws. He uses cross section of a log for his knife and tomahawks. He confesses he doesn't spend much time with either but feels he should "to keep the muscles fit."

Jeff also throws spike and star shurikens. He throws the ½" square by 7" long miefu-shinkage ryu shuriken with no-spin from 8 to about 24 feet. He also throws the shuriken with a half-spin and controls the rate of turn so that there are no multiple turns—just the same half-spin with a slower rate of turn. He says, "If you think about it, at the longer distances, the shuriken is pointed toward the target for a longer length of time. So, I think that the probability of a stick also increases."

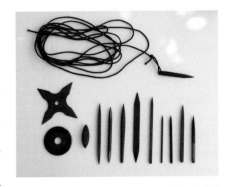

FIGURE 139.

Darts and shurikens that Jeff makes and markets–The rope dart (left, top) originated in China. Immediately to the right of the circular disc is the Chinese steel olive. At extreme right is the 5" long, $5/16$" across hexagonal dart that has become Jeff's favorite and which he throws with no-spin from as far as 30 feet. This author is a proud owner of all the darts and shurikens shown.

Jeff's first throwing knife was called a "Malayan throwing dagger" and came with an instruction sheet. Since then the books and videos he has collected have only confirmed what he learned by experimentation.

Jeff has advice for beginners including "Prepare to move fast." Fast does not necessarily mean throwing a knife—but ducking one. He had a knife come back at him that cut his arm open. It was thrown by someone else. He says, "the more practice the better. Be patient. Be persistent."

Jeff considers knife throwing a solitary activity. He does not belong to any knife throwing association but competes against himself. He says, "to maintain one's enthusiasm is the most difficult challenge. I rarely throw with other people. People who are serious about throwing are few and far between."

Jeff approaches the throwing of darts, shurikens, steel balls, flat discs, and coins from a combat point of view. Hence, when he practices, he never throws his last weapon "so it is a habit that I always have a weapon for that ultimate reality last ditch throw." But of course, he can carry five darts up his sleeve.

FIGURE 140.

The author with a set of Jeff Adams' five darts vertically mounted on his belt.

Despite an occasional miss, Jeff is able to hit a 2" circle from 30 feet consistently. Jeff had been throwing for 45 years but never had any complaint from his neighbors even if he sometimes throws as early as 6:00 in the morning. It must be that good throwers make good neighbors.

JOHN L. BAILEY

John fondly recalls, "One extraordinary day, many summers ago, my Dad took a chance and cast off the so-called parent code of conduct role either by accident, design, or desperation, I will never know. I did not realize it at the time that it was going to be this side of him that would bond a father and son for life.

"I had a bit of an attitude then because I thought that all other kids in the neighborhood had their dads out shooting hoops, throwing a football, or fielding flies. My dad did not go in for that much as he was built like a fireplug and was not one for chasing a ball around. I really wanted that sort of father and son stuff. Not that he wasn't a great dad. I just wanted something that we could do together. So it came as quite a surprise when he called me over to the side of the barn one day, where I thought he was clearing weeds and said, "When I was your age my dad was already in his sixties and had little time or energy to play with me. But back then, boys found fun wherever they could and out of whatever they found. So this is what I did to entertain myself.

"Before I could figure out what on earth he was driving at, he slipped a strange looking knife from his back pocket, turned and threw it towards the barn; firmly imbedding it in the center of a freshly drawn chalk circle. It was still shaking its rusty blunt end at us when he turned and put his hand on my shoulder. 'I first learned to throw knives when I was about your age. Do you want to learn?' To which my first thought was MY DAD THROWS KNIVES? WOW! That summer I learned responsibility and diligence; how to hit the broad side of a barn and how to have hours and hours of fun."

For the longest time, John just threw for fun and like everyone else he would get frustrated when one day he could throw well and the next day he couldn't. So, sometimes, he never knew if he was going to get any better. However, he did get better. Better enough to throw around human targets. John throws right handed, overhand, primarily with half- or one and a half-spins.

John not only learned knife throwing but also inherited the knack for making knives from his dad who made his two first throwing knives from old lawn mower blades. John's talent for

FIGURE 141.

John was inducted into the IKTHOF in 2003 as International Instructor of the Year. He holds the Guinness book record in 2008 for the fastest speed and accuracy with the bullwhip. John, at one time, nailed a rattlesnake to the ground from 20 feet that was about to strike at a soldier under his charge.

designing and making knives did not escape the attention of the German knife company Boker. John has become the principal throwing knife designer for Boker Germany and Boker USA, whose knives are sold all over the world. He has designed the Starlight, Tan-Kri, Mini Bo-Kri, Biel-Ax, Ziel, and Ziel II for Boker.

Prior to becoming a professional, John estimates that he would have thrown at least 1,000,000 times. He throws approximately 7000 "pointy" objects around his assistant annually, not including practice. John throws bayonets, tomahawks, shurikens, and many custom axes and knives in his shows. His favorite throwing knife is the Ziel II. As an impalement artist, in his shows, he aims his knives around two targets: one that is 5 feet wide and 6 feet high; the other, 4 feet wide and 5 feet high.

John competes and has won championships from the IKTA and PKT. In one of these competitions, John recounts an experience that wasn't necessarily a bad thing but that was awfully annoying. He recalls, "I had a long-distance knife throwing competition in the bag, when I went to throw my knife (on which I had tried a new type of handle made from shrink tubing). The blade slipped completely out of the handle and missed the target by about 15 feet and I was still holding the handle in my hand. However, no one was exposed to any danger because of the type of competition it was: long-distance throwing, over an open field."

John has done shows in Estonia and in Germany. He has made TV appearances and did shows in church functions, sportsman dinners, and store openings. When parents attend his shows, he draws from his experience of spending hours of fun throwing with his father and his mom's gentle admonition for his speech.

John tells them, "I will not put shoulder pads or kneepads on your son. I will not put a helmet on his head. I will not have any kid 80 pounds heavier try to tackle him. No one will be throwing a ball at him or swinging a bat over his head. No one will be sliding in at him with cleats on their shoes, or kicking him in the shins as they're chasing after a ball. He won't even have to wear a cup. All I will do is hand him a knife and tell him, 'If you really want to please me, you will throw this knife away...at that target. If you really like me, and want to please me, you will throw it at that target all day.'"

He continues, "The point I'm trying to make here is half the time the knife is never in his hand. And when a mother or father say they're worried about him throwing the knife at his little playmates then I tell them if your son is prone to hitting kids with a hockey stick then don't give him a knife because he just might throw it at a kid. But if he has no problem interacting with other children and knows how to follow rules, then you shouldn't have any problem with him taking up the sport of knife throwing."

His knives, his videos, his shows, and the Bailey Backspin (a throw where he gives the knife a backspin with his index finger) are John's major contributions to the sport and art of knife throwing. Some of his students have gone on to break world records and have performed on television and stage all over the world. One of the most successful is Dr. Michael Bainton. But he has one other contribution that stands out.

John founded the Starlight 1611 Crusaders Boys Club. In the backyard of the Starlight Baptist Church in Winter Springs, Florida, John instructs young boys in the throwing of knives and the cracking of whips with the goal of teaching them discipline, responsibility, and respect. While the boys' parents admit to feeling uneasy in the beginning, they only have praise for John now.

Perhaps, founding the Club is John's way of passing on the legacy of his father. On that day when his dad took him aside, some 57 years ago, John learned about responsibility and diligence.

MICHAEL J. BAINTON, PH.D.
(ALAMO)

Mike has black belts in Hap Ki Do, Kung Jung Mu Sul, and currently is the Grand Master of Ba Ki Do. He tested for his 10th degree on August 8, 2003. Mike has excellent empty hand techniques and one would assume that Mike wouldn't think twice about throwing a knife for self-defense for he can always fall back on his empty hands. However, when asked if he would do so, his response was, "Absolutely not. I throw at targets only." This should explain Mike's training regimen.

FIGURE 142.

Mike's favorite throwing knife is the Bowie. Mike has been inducted into the IKTHOF twice: in 2004 as National Knife Throwing Champion of the Year and in 2005 as International Knife Thrower of the Year.

Mike started throwing on February 9, 2002 with some Bud K 15-inch throwers. Mike throws overhand with his right hand only. He describes, "I throw with my left foot forward in a similar stance of left side out for the martial arts. I find that soft knees and a very relaxed body will allow me to hit the bull's-eye more often. I lean into the throw pointing my left knee at the target and follow through with my right arm coming straight over my shoulder ending up near my right knee." His throwing arm does not cross his torso.

Mike does not allow any knives less than 12 inches on his throwing range or less than 15 ounces as he feels they are dangerous implements. He has thrown mostly 20 to 30 ounce knives from 15 to 18 inches in length for mountain man competitions as well as conventional throwing. He found that heavier knives do not hurt his elbows and shoulder like the lighter ones do. He admits, "I have to work very hard to get a 15 ounce knife down range from 29 feet but throwing a heavy knife I can relax my body and let the knife do all the work."

Mike had good instructions from many famous knife throwers including John Bailey, Carl Geddes, Bob Pyle, and Che Che Whitecloud. Consequently, he didn't learn bad habits. Mike threw from 500 to 700 knives each day on training regimen he developed. He threw mostly five knives at five targets from six different distances for the first two to three years seven days a week. Mike is dedicated.

He has a throwing range with eight conventional targets with permanent distances and a total of six mountain men targets. Mike teaches knife throwing on a daily basis for his throwing team including Saturdays and most Sundays. He has 25 children on his team, ages 6 to 14 years, who throw in competitions both conventional and mountain man. He also teaches groups who come to his range to try throwing for group activities and companies who hire him to teach team building for their executives and management personnel.

Mike throws overhand with a hammer grip with his thumb on the side. He does not do any trick throws. He throws using the blade grip from 8, 15, and 21 feet and handle grip from 12, 19, and 23 feet. Distances are different of course with all of his thirty sets but are within one foot of the above-mentioned distances. He specializes in the overhand throw. He uses only heavy knives. He keeps his arm on the same side of his body before and after releasing the knife. He focuses his throwing for competition. This must be the secret to how Mike took 44 first places, a number of second, and a few thirds in IKTHOF competitions. He holds four World Championship titles and is in the 2008 *Guinness Book of World Records* for most world championships won in knife throwing.

Mike placed third in the IKTHOF World Championships held October 2008. He wished he had more training time but could not throw for a six month period because he was diagnosed with cancer in Spring 2008. He regrets he lost the competitive edge he used to have but plans to perfect the overhand throw in the next ten years.

Mike is the executive director of the IKTHOF. The IKTHOF holds six major tournaments throughout the United States and held the World Championships in 2003 and 2004 in Las Vegas, in 2005, 2006, and 2007 in Claremore, Oklahoma, and in 2008 in Austin, Texas.

Mike aims for the continued growth of knife throwing as a sport and is looking forward to future IKTHOF throwing championships. Mike is currently updating his website www.ikthof.com to better serve throwers in all parts of the globe.

BOBBY BRANTON

Harry K. McEvoy's *Knife Throwing A Practical Guide* (Tuttle Publishing, 1973) describes a good knife: "Not every knife is suitable for throwing. First and foremost is to have a knife that is properly balanced for throwing. Next in importance is weight, in proportion to balance and length, for the knife must have enough heft to enable it to penetrate and stick in the target. And finally, it must be long enough to give the knife thrower maximum control over his throw."

Bobby discovered Harry McEvoy in the 1980s, learned what quality throwers were like, and has been throwing regularly ever since. Bobby tried many of the knives on the market and found none that met his throwing style, so he decided to make them. He has been making knives and selling them through Branton Knives for the past 25 years.

Bobby has handcrafted knives for such greats as Paul LaCross and Che Che Whitecloud. He has also handcrafted knives for the former governor of South Carolina Carroll Campbell and the former President of the United States George W. Bush. Bobby's knives have been featured in most of the Knives annuals and in other publications such as *Knife World, Blade Magazine, Tactical Knives, Knives Illustrated,* and *South Carolina Wildlife.*

When Bobby was starting out early in his career, he met knife throwing legends Paul LaCross and Che Che Whitecloud. It was Paul LaCross who taught and motivated Bobby to become a professional knife thrower. He has since put together a throwing exhibition, which he performs throughout the Southeast with his wife as his assistant.

FIGURE 143.

Bobby Branton with the official throwing knife of AKTA. He was inducted into the IKTHOF in 2004 as Knife Thrower of the Year.

In 2005, Bobby was hired by a production company to be a technical advisor and to train actress Selma Hayek for a role in the movie "Bandidas." He was flown to Los Angeles to train Ms. Hayek for the role of a bank robber who happens to be an expert with knives. He was later flown to the movie set in Mexico City to further train Ms. Hayek and to act as a technical advisor during filming and then to Durango, Mexico where he performed the actual throwing on location for the more difficult throwing scenes. Bobby also designed and crafted some very special throwing knives for Miss Hayek and actor Sam Shepard to use in the film.

Bobby put on one of the first knife throwing competitions back in the early 1990s. He brought back to life one of the oldest and best-known knife throwing organizations, the AKTA, from extinction. Bobby is now the president of the AKTA, which under his leadership has held contests for 11 years, but had to cut back in 2007 due to personal obligations.

Bobby has been one of the biggest promoters of knife throwing as a competitor, as a teacher, as an impalement artist, as a knife designer and maker, and as a technical advisor.

Despite all his accomplishments, Bobby, takes greatest pride in the friendships he has formed over the years. In his words, "I have got to know and have been friends with all of the major professional knife throwers of our time."

JOSEPH "BROKENFEATHER" DARRAH

Joe used to open his circus act with a short bullwhip routine cracking and cutting lengthwise rolled up newspaper filled with confetti, because he could get a lot of cuts on the paper and each one came with a sonic boom and made it appear that the paper was exploding so when he starts cracking a bullwhip inside a tent the noise quiets the crowd and then they are ready to watch some knife throwing. He was a knife thrower for R&S Traveling Circus in 1978-1979.

Joe remembers, "My throwing started at the age of five when my father who was with the 101st Airborne taught me to throw M-3 trench knives and from then on I was hooked!" He has since been throwing for 45 years for which he was inducted into the IKTHOF four times.

Joe throws no-spin from 1½ and 15 feet, half-spin from 2 feet and as far as 60 feet and full-spin from 5 to as far as 70 feet. He throws overhand and underhand with both his hands and has a specialty—that of throwing the knife with his back to the target. Joe had done demonstrations where he cut flowers from a person's mouth with a sharp knife. He also has thrown five or six knives up a board and walked on them like a ladder to stand at the top of the board.

Joe does not only throw knives: he makes them. He says, "I like a dagger-type thrower as well as very small items that I usually make from scrap that I cut big knives out of and the steel just speaks to me, or I'll take a piece of steel and just start grinding away and it comes out as it will and I guess from years of doing it the weight and feel in my hands creates nice throwers almost of their own accord."

He has made knives for Che Che White Cloud, Dick Haines, Dr. David Adamovich, Dr. Mike Bainton, this author, and several martial arts schools. Joe does not make knives for money although he sells quite a few.

The crafting of a knife to Joe is a passion and he credits the late Harry McEvoy for most of what he knows about knife making. Joe has taught knife making to 20 people and 10 of them are still at it. He teaches knife making for free. Joe makes knives that are of such high quality that he was inducted into the IKTHOF as National Knife Maker of the Year in 2005.

Joe teaches defensive knife throwing using the blade grip. He makes his students stand with their back against the target then walk away and at any point between 2 feet and 18 feet he commands, "Throw!" They have to turn and throw the knife. He adds, "It teaches them to throw by reflex and to automatically judge the distance in a split second, that is why I feel that is probably the best defensive throw there is—plus the power you can apply is incredible!"

Joe is part Blackfoot Indian and is known as Brokenfeather in the knife throwing world. He has thrown knives, axes, tomahawks, shurikens, and even finishing nails more than 1,000,000 times. Joe favors the right overhand knife throw. As a test of his endurance, at one time, he threw 1,000 knives in 88 minutes. His farthest throw was from 178 feet sticking a knife into a 16" diameter target.

Joe says, "I never intended to become a tournament thrower. I just did it to get together with other knife throwers but have managed to win a few things." Joe started competing in 2002. Among the "few things" that he has won were seven world championships and more than 20 national IKTHOF championships. He had also won first places in WWAC, WKTG, PKT, and AKTA competitions.

Joe is a fierce competitor. When asked what was the worst thing that happened to him while throwing, his answer was, "Lost in a tournament."

FIGURE 144.
Brokenfeather stressing the importance of safety in knife throwing to young boys. Joe has done seminars on knife throwing and whip cracking and had taught several hundred people. He was awarded Master Instructor Knife and Tomahawk by the PKT (2004) and Thrown Weapons Instructor by the IKTHOF (2004). This author is the proud owner of the knife at the top.

SCOTT D. GRACIA

Scott is a good neighbor, not because his neighbor has a good fence but because he uses a bit of common sense and common courtesy. Scott says, "All my neighbors know me because I made a point to introduce myself. I told them about my website and what I did for a living. And, of course, I invited them over to throw a few when we first met. So instead of possibly being the crazy guy throwing knives and hawks in his backyard, I am the guy who their grandkids can't wait to come over and learn to throw knives and spears with."

He adds, "Don't throw for hours on end if you know all your neighbors are home, or if they are having a party or get together. Put yourself in their place, would you want to listen to their barking dog for hours on end? Give them only small doses of clanging/noise. However if you live in the country, call all your friends, turn up the radio, move back to about 50 feet and see who gets the first stick!"

Scott throws for fun but occasionally competes and at one time had to change his style of throwing to adjust to a longer distance that was used in the competition. He had to stretch his normal comfortable 11 feet throwing distance to 12 feet. So, he used a longer knife and changed his grip. He aims at concentric circles with a 2.5" bulls-eye, and 8" secondary ring and a 16" outer ring that are painted on 20-inch diameter log rounds when he practices for competitions.

Scott throws overhand with his left hand with half-spins from as far as 22 feet and full-spins from as far as 15 feet. The lightest he has thrown is a blow-gun dart; the heaviest, a 9-lb jackhammer drill bit that he threw from 11 feet. He says, "Anything farther than that, I really regret it the next day."

Scott has thrown knives, spears, and all kinds of pointed things, but he doesn't throw with no-spin. He explains, "I throw overhand, over my left shoulder. This is the most accurate way for me to throw. Some of the other ways look cool but I couldn't hit sand if I fell off a camel with those other techniques so I just stick with what works for me."

Scott has thrown close to 200,000 times and has had his share of close calls. So he advises, "For safety, move everything away from your throwing range that you like having. Knives always seem to ricochet into the things we like the most. Keep everything at least 20 feet behind the person throwing. Wear safety glasses."

He emphasizes, "Don't throw using all your might like a baseball pitcher. Let the weight of the knife do the work for you. Remember if you give it everything you've got when you throw...it can come back at you at just about the same speed."

Scott threw his first knife when he was 10 but really got serious about knife throwing in 1996. The Internet was a major factor. He started learning from people all over the world who sent lots of great information to his website including pictures, articles, target designs, knife designs, event info, tips, techniques etc. He acknowledges, "It was great. I got so much information I had no choice but to share it with everyone! Hence the throwzini.com website."

Despite recently having chemotherapy, Scott still squeezed in time to go to Austin, Texas and to San Diego, California to compete, meet like-minded folks, and "have a blast." He continues to attend to his throwzini.com website, which provides all sorts of information on the sport/art of throwing and sends a newsletter every two weeks to throwers located around the world—numbering more than 17,000. And growing.

B.

C.

A.

FIGURE 145.

Scott (A), his grip (B), his targets (C) and his favorite throwing knives (D). Scott was inducted into the IKTHOF in 2003 for Knife Throwing Promoter of the Year and in 2006 for the Pinnacle Award of Success.

D.

RICHARD L. HAINES
(THE DEAN OF GREAT THROWING)

Dick was six years old when he became interested in throwing knives while watching the 10 cent movies and seeing an act at a county fair. He then got into trouble for throwing his mom's butcher knives into his dad's favorite cherry tree.

Dick remembers, "My coordination early on was not very good." But he practiced, practiced, practiced, until he became one of the greatest throwers in the United States.

His practice had imprinted into Dick's neuromuscular memory an instinctive sense of distance. He has done some variety shows in which he was in the finale and his board was set almost at random and had to begin throwing immediately! He had no time to measure or step off the distance. This was when his target girl was already on the board and the stage was full of people dancing.

Dick was self-taught but had studied other throwers' styles. He can throw from over the left and right shoulders or from beside the right leg or left hip with either hand plus side arm under the leg, between the legs, cross throws, backwards or upside down. He has thrown while standing on a slack rope or from the tight wire. He has thrown from a rola-bola, through his own lariat loop, and at the Wheel of Death...sometimes all three at the same time!

Dick throws with both hands. When he throws with his right, his left foot is in front. When he throws with his left, his right foot is in front. For those who want to learn how to throw with both hands at the same time or with alternate hands, he advises, "You will learn faster and have much better success if your feet are placed to favor your most difficult side."

He says, "You can be a great thrower. But it will take practice, practice and practice. Keep throwing as long as you keep getting better. When you see no improvement—STOP! Practice another unrelated skill or just take a break. This way you will not be practicing bad habits. Then practice again, for as long as you can, but as soon as you quit improving STOP! Get the idea?"

Having been throwing professionally for many years, he has his share of "one of those days." He recalls, "We were doing a show at a festival in Pennsylvania. I was doing a short variety show. At the end of the show we did the knife act. During one of the poses at the knife board I hit the target girl in the top of the head with a knife handle. At the end of the show we then did the Wheel of Death. There wasn't even a knot on the girl's head.

After the show we walked around the festival grounds to see what all was going on. It started to rain. We thought that we wouldn't have to do the second show and the festival grounds were clearing out. There were only workers left.

We went back to the outdoor stage to load up to come home to Ohio and there they were, all of those people, sitting in the grass in the rain, waiting for the show. We figured that if we had to do the show in the rain we would make it a long one. I got out all of the magic stuff that would survive the rain, a balloon act complete with volunteers, nylon bull whips, Cherokee blowguns, the fire act including things that I hadn't done during the first show, and finally the knife throwing act that ran extra long. By this time people were sitting in water that was literally running down the hill. The stage manager ran up to me after the show and said, 'Do you know how much time you did?' I just answered, 'You didn't see anybody leave did you?'"

Dick would consider using his knife for self defense. He says, "I often walk past places that have pit bulls and they sometimes break their leash or fence. My youngest son was attacked within a block of our house and years after I was attacked on the next street over. My son had stitches, I did not. I always carry a knife of some sort but would not throw it unless I had another one at the ready."

Dick has designed and made some of his knives, tomahawks, axes, spears, atlatl, and other throwing implements. He advises to have water jet blanks if you are going to make your knives. He says, "They are smooth and not made softer on the edge from grinding to shape. If you use a grinder to put an edge on them, work slowly. They should never feel hot where you grind. This is for stock removal knives or after the blades has been hardened."

Dick has been throwing since 1942. He is still throwing and giving lessons—passing on the art of throwing to others.

FIGURE 146.

Dick Haines with his favorite 16-inch diamond point stage knife and the Wheel of Death. Dick was inducted into the IKTHOF for Golden Lifetime Achievement Award in 2004.

ROY HUTCHISON

Roy has been throwing knives since his boyhood days in England when he was in the local Scouts Group. He was about 13 years old at the time and one of the pieces of equipment that a scout was supposed to have was a knife.

Roy can't remember how he acquired his sheath knife. However, he remembers, "This knife was my pride and joy! This knife was my most treasured thing. I would polish the blade, the brass hilt, and the handle with my Dad's boot polish when he was not looking. The knife was never very far from me. I would take it to school, in my pocket, so as to look at it now and again, but to keep it away from the teachers' eyes or it would have been confiscated."

Roy got started throwing when he joined a group of schoolboys throwing their penknives at pieces of paper that were laying on the grass to see if they could stick them. He couldn't stick it into the ground because the handle was awkward to hold so he tried throwing from the blade and got some sticks at about 3 feet. And he got hooked! Soon, he was sticking from 4 to 5 feet away.

The war had only finished a few years before. There was an abundance of things to throw at. Doors and beams still standing, joists and all manner of wooden things. There were also lots of pointed things lying around like long nails, old kitchen knives, bits of metal that he was able to make a point on by rubbing on the kerbstones, etc. He recalls, "My friend Peter was not into throwing so he would wander around the site looking for bits and pieces, while I threw merrily away."

There was an occasion when he did something he considers really stupid. He narrates, "My friend Peter remembers it to this very day. We were out in the local park one day, climbing the trees and generally annoying the park keepers (climbing was not allowed). And I, as usual, was throwing my knives about at the trees.

"Peter was in a tree about 8 feet off the ground and I said to Peter, 'I'm going to stick my knife up the tree a bit, throw it back down for me.'

He said 'Don't hit me' or words to that effect. I threw the knife and I was about 2 feet too high. The knife thudded into his right leg! I can remember being worried about the trouble I was going to be in rather than the pain my friend was in.

"There was blood everywhere. We tied our handkerchiefs around his leg and struggled home. He told his Mum that he had fallen on something sharp (a true friend) and I believe he had stitches in the gash. He bears the scar to this very day. I never tried that trick again!"

Roy, now, has become an infinitely better thrower than when he aimed up the tree sixty years ago. Roy throws half-spin from as close as 3 feet and as far as 30 feet and full-spin from 10 and 40 feet. He throws right hand overhand focusing on the half-spin throw. He keeps no record but puts his stick rate at 99%. What is remarkable about Roy's half-spin throw is that he can throw from any distance and make the knife stick!

About two years ago, Roy was practicing in his garden and started thinking of the way he had been throwing. He had been happily half-spinning for 50 years and couldn't think of any reason why he has to alter his throwing method. Roy reasoned, "But I suppose it was because of all the new throwing friends that I have made, and met on the Internet, and exchanging ideas and listening to all the things that they do that I never knew existed. If I can throw a 30 foot half-spin, then I should be able to do at least a 12 foot no-spin or something similar."

Roy has no problem making knives because he owns a small engineering company that designs and manufactures steel components for firearms under license by various world companies. He says, "A knife is as aerodynamic as a house brick." He concluded, instinctively, that he needed a special kind of knife and new method of throwing if the knife is to stick in the no-spin throw. After going through many prototypes, he settled on one design: He came up with a

FIGURE 147.

Roy and knives that he designed for the half-spin throw.

14" long knife with a blade that is 1" wide blade and a ½" wide handle. The knife is ⅛" thick and weighed 13oz.

On the no-spin throw, Roy says, "I don't do much farther than 20 feet. In fact, I have no interest in that throw, except having it there as a bit of fun. No-spins are hard work, whereas half-spins are lazy and fun."

Roy is self-taught but is only too willing to share his half-spin and no-spin throwing methods with others who would like to learn how to throw. He has written about his throwing techniques in detail in Scott Gracia's website so much so that Scott calls him the "half-spin guru."

CHRIS S. KELLY

Chris feels that, "It is important for the serious thrower to fabricate his throwing implements for a number of reasons. It allows him to understand the basics of blade design and customize blades to better fit his throwing style. It enables him to fabricate his own designs and modify them until it melds with his hands (provided he has the necessary tools and machinery). As one idea leads to another, he will eventually come to understand the techniques of their use and the goals he wants to achieve with it."

From the time Chris started throwing things as a young boy he has always made most of his weapons, which included spears, slingshots, and knives. The first weapon that he threw was the spear because it was easy to make. As an adult he made his own throwing knives and spikes that led to his interest in shuriken-jutsu and in the throwing of the bo shuriken. As he studied the history of the art, he began to design and make his own shurikens.

Chris doesn't keep records of his sticks and misses but estimates that he has thrown spears, axes, knives, shovels, shakens and shurikens approximately

FIGURE 148.

Grip for the half-spin throw (left) and handle grip for the no-spin throw (right) that Chris uses on his favorite ½" square cross section 7½" long shuriken.

200,000 times. Chris has thrown most of his life but in the last five years had focused on throwing the bo shuriken. Occasionally, he pulls out his knives, tomahawks, shaken, and axes from storage and throws them.

Chris is basically self-taught, gleaning information from the internet and from the approximately 60 books in his collection that are mostly on shuriken-jutsu, hidden weapons, and the ninja arts. When he began his shuriken training in earnest, he sought the advice of experts like Jason Wotherspoon, Jeff Adams, and Houzan Suzuki.

Chris is left handed and throws overhand and underhand. He throws half-spin from 8 and 45 feet and full-spin from 8 and 19 feet. However, he has now focused his training on jikidahou or spinless throw and is able to hit his targets consistently from 6 to 40 feet. Like other no-spin throwers, he intends to throw no-spin from farther away.

He has adopted Ralph Thorn's suggestion of setting up two targets that face each other and spaced 30 feet apart. This arrangement allowed him to throw more and walk less. His first target is a grouping of 2" thick planks and Alder rounds, the whole unit being about 8 feet wide and 8 feet high. The planks are about 6 feet high and 10 inches wide. His second target is made of three 2-inch thick boards each 10 inches wide and 6 feet high. However, despite the width of his targets, occasionally, he still loses a dart because he throws close to a clump of bushes. He says that he doesn't easily forget a lost favorite dart.

Chris' injuries to date have been minor probably due to the precautions he takes when throwing. He wears safety glasses, wrist guards, long pants and good shoes when he throws. However, despite being safety conscious, Chris, at one time was cut when practicing a spinning shuriken throw devised by his son. Chris released the blade too early and it imbedded itself in the back of his calf, through the jeans he was wearing.

The thrower will do well to heed Chris' advice and wear long pants and wear a pair that you wouldn't mind getting holes in.

CYNTHIA MORRISON
(CINDINI)

One of the questions I asked Cynthia was, "What was the lightest implement you have thrown and what was the heaviest?" She wrote back, "The lightest would be a knife. The heaviest would be a spear not counting the 80 lb caber I turned in the Scotland Highland Games."

For some time, I paid no mind to her answer. When I was finishing her profile, I got more and more curious and emailed, "What events did you compete in?"

Cynthia holds the Florida State Records hammer and javelin throws (Women's class 30-35 years) in 1994 and the weight throw (Women's class 45-50 years) in 2005. She was Florida Sunshine State Champion in the javelin (Women's class 35-40 years) throw in June 2003. She was two-time national champion (1997 & 1998), 20 lb weight throw. She was the first woman to

FIGURE 149.

Cindini outlining a smiling Captain Olav with her knives.

compete in Scotland in the heavy athletics (turning the caber, stone throw, 28 lb weight throw, hammer throw) in 1994.

Cynthia has been throwing since 1997 starting with her favorite weapon, the spear, which she threw as part of her jousting involvement. She graduated to knife throwing in 2006 when she met her knife mentor the Great Throwdini (Dr. David Adamovich). It is no surprise that she took the stage name Cindini.

Cindini performs professionally with an impalement arts presentation including a human target as part of her sideshow. Other events of the show include sword swallowing, fire eating, walking on broken glass, lying on a bed of nails and a bed of machetes.

FIGURE 150.

Cynthia (left) was the American Jousting Association (AJA) international jousting champion in 1999 and 2000. Cynthia (right) throwing the javelin.

The transition from Cynthia to Cindini was not seamless. While Cynthia threw the spear where the arm crosses the torso after release, Cindini keeps her throwing arm at the same side of the body before and after release of the knife. While Cynthia aimed her spear at a target, Cindini had to throw her knives around her human target.

With her all-around throwing skills Cindini feels that her main contribution to the impalement arts is that of "keeping the performance part of knife throwing alive." That is why she wants to keep her human target smiling.

Michael does not have "one special motto" that he can share with beginning knife throwers. But he says, "I can give hints how to overcome special difficulties if somebody asks me.

"The only thing of real importance is your attitude. Nearly everybody can learn everything to a certain extent. But how far and quick you can go is very individual. If you accept this, the only thing you need is patience, time and practice. For a lot of people it is hard to understand that there is not a special trick how to hold the knife, but the need to develop skill and sensitivity for that special movement, and this needs individual time for everyone."

Michael uses the juggling of balls to illustrate a beginner's learning curve. He says, "Juggling three balls can be learned within three days. But juggling 4 or more balls takes between 6 to 24 months. Very few learn to juggle 6 or more balls. But if you don't start you will never know. OK, knife throwing is not that difficult, so I am pretty sure everybody can learn it if he does not care how long it takes and always strives to improve a little bit. While learning, you will have periods of good, steady progress, long plateaus, sometimes regress, and also sudden big jumps to higher skill. These are enjoyable and frustrating experiences at the same time."

Michael is a juggler. Thus, he has a very well coordinated left hand. However, he throws most of the time with his right hand only. He does not have any unique throw, "only the old fashioned overhand throw."

Being a master of spin-control in the overhand throw, he can throw from 4 meters with half-spin, one full-spin, one and a half-

FIGURE 151.

Michael Pahl.

spins, or two full-spins. He can also throw from 6 meters with half-spin, one full-spin, one and a half-spins, two full-spins, two and a half-spins, three full-spins, and so on. Essentially, he is able to throw and hit from any distance and has no special sweet points.

The longest distance Michael throws with a knife is 12 meters; with an axe, 14 meters. He can hit a 50 cm diameter target from 10 meters and consistently had placed either first, second or third in European throwing competitions. His training targets have no marks; instead he aims at small points in the natural structure of the wood.

Michael started knife throwing when he was 8 years old, throwing folders and kitchen knives but only did it from time to time. He started to learn knife throwing seriously about 10 years ago at the age of 39. He started to learn axe throwing some years later but did not find it worthwhile to train because it was so easy for him compared to knife throwing. He competes in axe throwing but still never trains in it.

The main obstacle Michael experienced at the beginning was a lack of training site. He lived in an apartment with no garden. It was difficult for him to find a suitable site where he could set up a target. It was also difficult to find good knives. He says, "All they sold in Germany was crap for children, but it is better now. This was not really an obstacle but maybe an advantage because starting with bad knives gave me great skill in even handling those." Where Michael lives now, he has a cellar in which he can throw, even from 6 meters.

On being asked if anything bad ever happened to him in his knife throwing career, he says, "No, but once I witnessed something funny during a competition in France. It was the long distance competition; we were sitting about 20 meters away from the target. One competitor stood at the 14 meter mark and threw his Swiss bayonet. He failed and the knob (lock) at the end of the handle broke and came back straight at us as fast as bullet and crashed into the wall only 20 cm away from my friends head."

DALMO MARIANO DA SILVA JR.

Dalmo started throwing kitchen knives and knives made from saw blades when he was 9 years old. At that young age, he never had any personal instructions and learned by teaching himself.

"I started self-teaching, but I could not go farther than half-spin. I did not realize that you needed to throw from different distances depending on how you hold the knife: by the blade or by the handle. I never did well so I threw knives when I felt like it and never got serious about it until I found people who could teach me. My real beginning started when I was around 40 years old, when I found the first real knife to throw."

Unfazed by the lack of teachers in Brazil, he searched for teachers outside its boundaries. Eventually, he found Ed Sachs, Lee Fugatt, Joe Darrah, Dr. David Adamovich, and other fine American throwers—on the Internet—from whom he learned the principles of knife throwing.

"Even after having e-learning lessons I could not know whether I was good or not. I had doubts as to how good a thrower I can become. I had no throwers to compare myself with in Brazil. Then I recorded some stunts and sent them to Dr. David Adamovich. When he said I was good, I became so self-confident that I started to throw better and better in a very short time." To supplement his e-learning, Dalmo collects books and videos about knife throwing.

"As I live in Brazil, I only had the opportunity to compete in online competitions with American throwers. I also compete with my fellow throwers from the IKTHOF and WFKT." Dalmo also competes in tournaments that he organizes in Brazil.

Dalmo does not keep records but he believes that over 44 years, he has thrown knives, tomahawks, bo shurikens, shakens, machetes, needles, spikes, big nails, scissors, screwdrivers, steel debris, and many other objects between 500,000 to 1,000,000 times. The lightest object he threw indoors was a big sewing needle with foam as a target; the heaviest he threw outdoors was an old German ax weighing a little over 3 kg.

Dalmo favors throwing knives or tomahawks depending on his mood. He also likes to throw the much lighter spike shurikens because they are tricky to throw and are very good learning tools. He throws half-spin (from 6, 12, 18 and 24 feet, full-spin (from 9, 15, and 21 feet) and no-spin (from 2 to 17 feet). He can stick consistently from as far as 50 feet.

Dalmo usually throws with his lead foot opposite to the hand that holds the knife, allowing a more powerful throw and good body balance. However, in throwing competitions, he throws with his right foot forward to "shorten" his distance to the target to compensate for rules that makes him throw too far in the back direction from his "natural" distance in multiple spins.

Dalmo has a full set of IKTHOF and WFKT targets in his backyard where he throws alone, with friends, or students. He has a portable target that he carries in his car for teaching people in other places. Dalmo teaches at a Circus School in São Paulo, a city around 70 km from his home where his students concentrate on avoiding hitting a human target. At the other end of the throwing spectrum, he has some students who are in the Brazilian Army whose main interests are in defensive knife throwing—hitting a human target.

Dalmo says that you cannot be too careful when you throw knives. Serious injury could result from a badly thrown knife that could bounce off the target in an unpredictable way. In one instance, Dalmo, could have gotten hit in the face by a bouncing knife if not for his quick reflexes. He was able to cover his face with his hand and luckily the knife did not hit point first. He says, "I never threw again without wearing safety goggles."

Dalmo designs and fabricates five models of throwing knives as well as kitchen, hunting, and tactical knives. He is rightfully proud of his Faka, a throwing knife that he designed and fabricated, that won in the last European knife throwing championships.

Dalmo was the opening act in the Festival de Circo do Brasil, a big international circus event, for his featured friend Dr. David Adamovich which

FIGURE 152.

Dalmo and the handle grips he uses on his Faka.

attracted more than 1,000 spectators, among them the mayor of Recife, and which generated a lot of media attention. Dalmo has performed in TV shows and had been featured in Brazilian magazines.

Keenly aware of the importance of an organization to the popularization of knife throwing, Dalmo organized the Associação Brasileira de Arremessadores de Facas (ABAF) the Brazilian Association of Knife Throwers. The ABAF is Dalmo's gift to Brazilian and perhaps South American knife and weapons throwers.

Dalmo may not become a household name in Brazil for he is competing with soccer names such as Pele and Ronaldo, with the Gracies of jiu-jitsu, and with the legendary Bimba of capoeira. However, there is no doubt that his name will become enshrined as the Father of Brazilian knife and weapons throwing. Indeed, it will be more apt to call him Father of South American Knife and Weapons Throwing.

HOUZAN SUZUKI

One of the questions I asked Houzan was, "What distances have you thrown from?" Houzan's answer is shown below.

Type of Throw	Implement	Closest	Farthest
Half-spin (blade grip)	Bo-Shuriken	5m	18m
Full-spin (handle grip)	Bo-Shuriken	5m	18m
No-spin (handle grip)	Bo-Shuriken	2m	18m

One other question I asked was, "What sort of obstacles did you have to hurdle to become good at throwing?" Houzan answered, "There was not a practice field. Good textbook was not found. There was not good throwing manufacture."

Houzan sent me his first videotape on shuriken throwing about a year ago as a gift. At the time, he lived in an apartment in a neighborhood of Mt. Fuji. There was some sort of a trellis in his backyard. The lack of practice field did not deter Houzan from throwing the shuriken. He threw through his doorway! To the left of his wooden target was his bench grinder.

Throwing to clear the trellis and the door had resulted in Houzan's unique throwing motion. He throws the shuriken at a low trajectory to clear the trellis then the door which only means that he has to throw with a greater speed than if he had more head room. He also had to throw in a near vertical motion to clear the sides of the door.

He wrote a book on the shuriken which he recently revised and produced two DVDs. The second of his DVDs showed him throwing shuriken-type throwers at his sword-wielding training partner.

Houzan collects books, videotapes, and throwing implements. Aside from his favored shuriken, he throws the knife, sword, spear, scissors, and machine shop tools such as screwdrivers. The lightest implement he has thrown is the needle of a blowgun dart.

What did Houzan do about the third obstacle "There was not good throwing manufacture?" He made them.

FIGURE 153.

Houzan designs and fabricates shurikens and gives them a finish by coating them with oil and then fires them.

FIGURE 154.

The bulbous handles of these shurikens are designed for the no spin throw.

Despite the obstacles that he had to overcome, Houzan has become an exceptional shuriken thrower. Look at his throwing distances in the table presented above. He throws full-spin from as far as 18m. That is not uncommon. He throws half-spins from as far as 18 meters. That is not uncommon. He throws no-spin from as far as 18 meters.That is extraordinary!!

I "met" Houzan when he invited me to become a member of an internet forum that he manages. The common thread that links its members is the no-spin throw.

Houzan considers the forum which he calls "theoretical organization about no-spin throw" as his major contribution to the art of throwing. Houzan communicates with the forum members using a computer translator and occasionally a friend who speaks English.

Two books, two DVDs, and thousands of throws later, Houzan has not forgotten the lessons he learned at the beginning of his throwing career. He says, "As a beginner do not throw forcefully. You must select a throwing implement that is easy to throw. Throw responsibly. Do not throw too close to the target to avoid dangerous knife bounce backs."

Houzan is the founder of the mumyou ryu school of shuriken throwing. He used a secret formula on his way to becoming the world's foremost exponent of the no-spin shuriken. He used the obstacles that confronted him as stepping stones.

JOHN TAYLOR

You can call John two other names that will put a smile on his face: Little John and Conejomatar. The first one is easy to explain. He lives in Yorkshire, England and people associate his name to the tales of Robin Hood. But he is not so little. He is 6'4".

Conejomatar is one name that you would normally not call an Englishman. I asked him, "How did you get the name rabbit killer?"

"I was given the name while on a holiday in Spain a few years ago. Over in England rabbits are a real pest. Over the years I have shot thousands for the gamekeepers and farmers. My farthest shot with my customized rifle was 458 yards."

FIGURE 155.

(Left) John and his English teammate, Rich Sunderland, at the Alamo, 2008. (Right) Confidence is one of the traits that John has plenty of. In the background is John's van as he throws a knife with his back to the target.

John had to hurdle a number of obstacles on his way to becoming a highly competitive knife thrower. He says, "The first hurdle was that I was a Police Officer and it was not the done thing to be throwing. So, when I retired, I dabbled with it and then it really hooked me about two years ago. It was easy for me to construct a range as I help out at a local paintball center and the owners let me use the facilities whenever I want. Another hurdle I had to overcome in England was to find good throwing knives as they are not readily available to buy over here so I started making my own. Plus a further hurdle I had, over here in England, was that once I decided to get serious about throwing I was completely on my own and had nobody to learn from or discuss techniques with."

John was self-taught when he started throwing years ago and has only progressed to serious throwing in the past couple of years. A big influence in his throwing was the DVD by Dr. David Adamovich. An even greater influence was the tuition he had from Joe Darrah over the past couple of years.

FIGURE 156.

John (top) framed against a very much thrown at IKTHOF target. John was inducted into the IKTHOF in 2006 for International Achievement Award. Two of the several grips that John uses in the overhand throw (middle, bottom).

Joe "Brokenfeather" Darrah, in an email to this author said, "John had progressed quite a bit." A bit?

In two years, only, of tournament throwing, John has reached both Expert in knife and tomahawk throwing under the IKTHOF rules. As icing on the cake, John says, "I came second at the Frontiersman throw at the Alamo this year (2008)."

John played a small part in a nationwide drama called *Heartbeat*, where he played the part of a Turkish knife thrower in a pantomime. Most recently, he has just finished filming for the History Channel on the throwing of an African knife. He is teaching scout leaders whom he hopes will teach scouts. He had also been hired to teach a leading actor to throw knives in a production of Shakespeare's Othello.

John, who throws knives, axes, tomahawks, screwdrivers, scissors, shuriken, shaken, machetes, and spikes is an avid collector of books, videos, and throwing implements. He says, "Anything out there that I can buy and learn from, it's mine."

John started throwing as a child playing knife games and he distinctly remembers throwing a 10" Bowie when he was 10 years old. He began serious knife throwing three years ago and has "worn a path in our lovely lawn" on his way to becoming an Expert knife and tomahawk thrower.

John says, "I am trying to promote knife throwing here in the UK and as such have a throwing club with just a few members who meet on a monthly basis. But the addiction of throwing is spreading over here, some day we will hold a tournament. Plus I am involved with a throwing site on the net based in the UK. I am very keen to teach others how to throw."

He adds, "There are no throwing organizations yet in the UK but I intend to remedy that in time."

CHRISTIAN THIEL

Christian started throwing knives when he was 16, learning the basics from books written in German, English, and French. Six years later, he got a personal throwing lesson from John Bailey (they met in the knife-town of Solingen), giving him a head start and incentive to train more regularly. In the following years he learned much about throwing from the online articles which the people around Matthew Rapaport and Tim Valentine had produced, and started a website on the topic in German language to fill the information gap in his country.

In the first few years, he felt that he experimented too much, always gleaning tips and quirks from other throwers at the European competitions. Now he has found his personal style, with only one major change in the last few years: "Visiting Dr. David Adamowich, I found his throwing technique quite similar to mine, and learned to emphasize the effortlessness of the motion. But I could never do it as fast as him."

FIGURE 157.
Christian Thiel

Christian's favorite throwing knife is the Faka that was designed and is produced by Dalmo Mariano from Brazil. He throws his knives, right handed, half-spin from 2.5 meters and 6 meters, full-spin from 3 meters and 7 meters and no-spin from a maximum distance of 3.5m.

FIGURE 158.

Group photo from the Big European Throwers Meeting 2007 in Erlangen, Germany. Some of the regular top throwers and organizers are: (1) Christian Thiel (Germany), (2) Fery Olbort (Czech Republic), (3) Christian Buttarello (France), (4) Norbert Maier (Germany), (5) Michael Pahl (Germany), (6) Dieter Führer (Germany), (7) Hombre Andel (Czech Republic), (8) Dominique Gagnon (France), (9) Frank Salonius (Finland), (10) Philippe Catania (France), (11) Michel Dujay (France), (12) Tomas Maurer (Czech Republic), (13) Gregor Paprocki (Germany), (14) Kari Salonius (Finland), (15) Peter Kramer (Germany), (16) Sigrid Hansen (Germany), (17) Gabriela Beckmann (Germany) and (18) Piotrek Stachera (Poland).

Being a city dweller, Christian initially lacked a decent training area, but has since set up a sturdy target out in the countryside. It is not marked, instead he aims at spots in the wood, which increases the life of the target and promotes flexibility. He does not use human figures for targets because he said, "I would never throw a knife for self-defense reasons, even in dire conditions."

Christian feels that his major contribution to the throwing arts are his websites (English: www.KnifeThrowing.info, German: www.Messerwerfen.de) that provide easily accessible details on knife throwing techniques and related topics, networking the throwers in Europe and providing them with a stable community platform. Christian considers, "This is the achievement and challenge closest to my heart." And judging from the number of website visitors, close to 450,000 since inception, people really appreciate his effort.

Early on, through his online forum and together with Norbert Maier, Christian kick-started a throwing community in Germany that has since spread in Europe. In 2002, he was deeply involved with the creation of the European umbrella association for knife throwers, the European Throwing Club "Flying Blades" (EuroThrowers), of which he since is the elected vice-president. The club organizes, each year in a different country, the "Big European Throwers Meeting," the biggest knife throwing event on the continent.

There were parallel developments in knife and axe throwing in the Czech Republic, France, Germany, and Italy. However, in many competitions, the rules used were different. This changed in September 2008, when eight representatives of the sport from the different countries came together in the town of Chomutov, Czech Republic to discuss common rules. After three hours of negotiations (which Christian chaired) in four languages, they agreed on a standard set of European Knife Throwing and Axe Throwing Rules to be used in international competitions.

ERIC THORNBURG

Eric's father died before he started throwing knives. But he remembers, "My father was an excellent baseball pitcher who snapped a man's arm with a fastball and once killed a rabbit with a rock thrown from something like 200 feet." Eric has good throwing genes.

Eric had been throwing knives, swords, bayonets, shuriken spikes and other improvised weapons such as screwdrivers for 25 years and while entirely self-taught in his younger days, he had picked up some important things from people he met over the internet. He throws half-spin from as far as 50 feet, full-spin (underhand only) from as far as 70 feet and no-spin from zero to 40 feet.

Eric has dozens of targets and no two are the same. He prefers to throw at round poles set into the ground because they best simulate a human opponent, and can be thrown at easily from all angles. However, he also uses flat boards and sometimes logs. As far as dimensions go, he prefers to have a target area that is the size of a man's torso: about two feet high, three feet off the ground, and about a foot wide.

Virtually everything that Eric has ever done with knife throwing has been with the self-defense or survival aspect somewhere in his mind. Thus, his answer came as no surprise when I asked him, "Are you involved in any martial arts?"

Eric's answer was, "The only martial art I am currently involved in is my form of knife throwing." Thus, Eric founded a martial art that has an identity all its own: It is based on the no-spin throw and on a specific style of throwing.

The no-spin throw is the foundation of Eric's martial arts school of knife throwing. It is simple in concept because a knife in the no-spin throw will always be pointing to the front before and after release and therefore the possibility of hitting with the point could be as high as 99%. In contrast, in the half-spin and in the full-spin throw, there are windows in time where the knife could be pointed other than toward the target. Such a knife could hit flat or hit with its butt.

He explains, "My no-spin style is different from the shuriken style of no-spin in that it emphasizes wrist action to propel the knife, which allows the thrower to throw from more angles than traditional shuriken throwers can, and also appears to give better mobility and power to the thrower. That, I am convinced,

FIGURE 159.

Eric jumps over
a chair throwing
a knife (left). Eric
throws swords (right)
from as far as 60 feet
aiming at tree trunks.

makes my style the most effective style of weapons throwing for actual hand to hand combat."

The no-spin throw is, simultaneously, advanced because there is a need to suppress the spin of the knife by pushing down on its tail at the time of release. Thus, it is not a natural throw compared to the half and the full-spin throws where the thrower releases the knife at the proper time and lets nature do its work.

Eric's school of knife throwing is not unlike Japanese shuriken-jutsu where a school specializes in a particular aspect of shuriken throwing. It is also similar in concept to the hidden weapons of China where a school could be known for a unique throwing weapon that in turn entails the use of a particular throwing style such as in the throwing of the Chinese flying dart.

Eric, like all accomplished knife throwers, searched for a knife design that suits his throwing style and the purpose of his throws. He recently discovered a new, more precise method for balancing and making knives that he is excited about. He says, "I now know how to locate the balance point of a knife at 38 percent from the back of the handle to minimize spin; and the way to do this without putting handles on the knives is to put holes in the blade." The result was the shurknife.

With the shurknife, that 99% sticking average could very well become 99.8%—or better.

FIGURE 160.

Eric corroborated with
Chris Kelly on the design
and fabrication of the
shurknife. This author
is a proud owner of the
shurknife.

REFERENCES

Claude Blair, *The Complete Encyclopedia of Arms and Weapons*, Simon & Schuster, 1982, New York, New York.

Peter Brancazio, *Sport Science*, Simon & Schuster, 1984, New York, New York.

Douglas H. Y. Hsieh, *Ancient Chinese Hidden Weapons*, Meadea Enterprises Co., Inc., 1986, Republic of China.

Shirakami Ikku-ken, *Shuriken-Do*, Paul H. Crompton Ltd., 1987, London, England.

Amante P. Mariñas Sr., *Pananandata Guide to Knife Throwing*, United Cutlery Corp., 1999, Sevierville, Tennessee.

Harry K. McEvoy, *Knife Throwing A Practical Guide*, 1973, Charles E. Tuttle Company, Inc., Rutland, Vermont.

W.G. McLean & E. W. Nelson, *Schaum's Series Theory and Problems of Engineering Mechanics*, McGraw-Hill Book Company, 1988, New York, New York.

ABOUT THE AUTHOR

Amante P. Mariñas, Sr., teaches pananandata, his family's fighting system, which he was introduced to when he was eight years old by his granduncle Ingkong Leon Marcelo. Mariñas holds black belts in shorin-ryu karate from the Commando Karate Club under Sensei Latino Gonzalez and Sensei Anselmo "Pop" Santos and in aikido from the Philippine Aikido Club under Sensei Ambrosio Gavileno.

He has written over 100 articles and is the world's most published practitioner of Filipino martial arts. He has authored eleven other books including *Arnis de Mano, Arnis Lanada, Pananandata Knife Fighting, Pananandata Yantok at Daga, Pananandata Dalawang Yantok, Pananandata Rope Fighting, Pananandata Guide to Knife Throwing, Pananandata Guide to Sport Blowguns,* and *Pananandata: Its History and Techniques.*

Mariñas designed the VM Bulalakaw, which is marketed by United Cutlery Corporation. He has also designed and fabricated bagakays, other knives, axes, spears, and many-pointed throwing implements.

Mariñas is originally from Pambuan, a small village in Gapan, Nueva Ecija, in Central Luzon in the Philippines. He taught chemical engineering at Adamson University in Manila before coming to the United States. Today he lives in Fredericksburg, Virginia, with his wife, Cherry. His son, Amante Jr., is heir to pananandata.